To Joyce, ~ March 6th, 2019

D0832017

CHOOSING
*R*EST

CULTIVATING A SUNDAY HEART
IN A MONDAY WORLD

SALLY BREEDLOVE

NAVPRESS

Bringing Truth to Life
P.O. Box 35001, Colorado Springs, Colorado 80935

OUR GUARANTEE TO YOU

We believe so strongly in the message of our books that we are making this quality guarantee to you. If for any reason you are disappointed with the content of this book, return the title page to us with your name and address and we will refund to you the list price of the book. To help us serve you better, please briefly describe why you were disappointed. Mail your refund request to: NavPress, P.O. Box 35002, Colorado Springs, CO 80935.

The Navigators is an international Christian organization. Our mission is to reach, disciple, and equip people to know Christ and to make Him known through successive generations. We envision multitudes of diverse people in the United States and every other nation who have a passionate love for Christ, live a lifestyle of sharing Christ's love, and multiply spiritual laborers among those without Christ.

NavPress is the publishing ministry of The Navigators. NavPress publications help believers learn biblical truth and apply what they learn to their lives and ministries. Our mission is to stimulate spiritual formation among our readers.

ISBN 1-57683-292-9

Cover design and photo by Steve Eames
Creative Team: Nanci McAlister, Greg Clouse, Amy Spencer, Glynese Northam

Some of the anecdotal illustrations in this book are true to life and are included with the permission of the persons involved. All other illustrations are composites of real situations, and any resemblance to people living or dead is coincidental.

Unless otherwise identified, all Scripture quotations in this publication are taken from the HOLY BIBLE: NEW INTERNATIONAL VERSION® (NIV®). Copyright © 1973, 1978, 1984 by International Bible Society. Used by permission of Zondervan Publishing House. All rights reserved. Other versions used include *The Message: New Testament with Psalms and Proverbs* (MSG) by Eugene H. Peterson, copyright © 1993, 1994, 1995, used by permission of NavPress Publishing Group.

Breedlove, Sally, 1950-
  Choosing rest : cultivating a Sunday heart in a Monday world / Sally Breedlove.
     p. cm.
Includes bibliographical references.
  ISBN 1-57683-292-9
  1. Rest--Religious aspects--Christianity. 2. Christian life. I.
Title.
  BV4597.55 .B74 2002
  248.4'6--dc21
                                    2002003873

Printed in the United States of America

1 2 3 4 5 6 7 8 9 10 / 06 05 04 03 02

FOR A FREE CATALOG OF
NAVPRESS BOOKS & BIBLE STUDIES,
CALL 1-800-366-7788 (USA)
OR 1-416-499-4615 (CANADA)

For Steve
my beloved and my friend
Song of Songs 5:16

Contents

Foreword

MY FATHER, A MEDICAL MISSIONARY AND CONFERENCE SPEAKER, always super-charged with energy and enthusiasm, would often prod my brother and me with an aphorism such as, "It's better to burn out than to rust out for God." Bestowed with a generous portion of my father's genes, I find the idea of burning out preferable to the prospect of rusting out. Fortunately, between the extremes of burning and rusting lies another option—the way of resting in God.

Rest. Isn't it a wonderful word? Wouldn't it be great to experience rest of body and peace of heart without all the urgent needs and crises of modern civilization? Wouldn't we all like to be free from such frantic, unceasing activity? Yet sometimes rest seems an unachievable goal.

So when I first opened the pages of this book I experienced a jolt, which left me with an uneasy feeling, as if I'd just received news about something I should have known all too well, but had forgotten, or disregarded.

It wasn't exactly guilt that I felt, but a wry feeling of regret. And I've learned through many years that such uneasiness is often salutary, like a highway sign that informs me I'm going north instead of west, but also points me back in the direction I *thought* I was heading, after somehow having gotten off track.

I think most of us, especially those who have held Jesus in our hearts for many years, believing that we were ardently following him (just look at all the ministries we are involved in!), have a lot to learn about such pointers, the road signs of our souls. I've become convinced that most of us, in the more mature stages of our lives, need freshening. Our centrally held faith needs to be lived out from a new angle. We yearn to experience renewal. We wonder if it might feel like being born again, *again.*

In this beautifully proportioned book, Sally Breedlove not only leads us through many of the issues and problems faced by Christian believers of our time but speaks personally of the way God has led her into renewal and peace.

I'm a poet, and an idea for a poem may well occur for me on the fly; a fleeting image or connection arrives and feels significant enough to be scribbled in my ever-present journal. But to follow that image into the heart of truth, to wait for the poem, and the Spirit that speaks through it as it is developed, as it is revealed to me, requires more than a jotting in a journal. It requires quiet, undeviating focus. It calls me to listen for the Spirit's voice, to pay attention to the creation and the Creator, to serve the gift and follow the Word. This cannot happen when there is distraction.

In this book my imagination was charged, magnetized by Sally Breedlove's mention of two gardens—the beautiful, unspoiled one called Eden, where the human race was given an amazing opportunity to begin something new with God, for God, in relationship with Him, and the garden we're heading toward, with its River of Life and its green, healing trees where all nations and peoples will be healed of rivalries and long-standing feuds. We've left Eden behind, with its primal beauty and peace. We are in the hiatus of a confused and frustrated time in history, when peace and healing seem remote. We hold onto that hope with the slender string of faith that sometimes threatens to snap.

Green, in all its verdant varieties, has always been my signal-color. I live and write beside a ravine with a rushing stream with banks of ferns and a stand of cedar trees that lives out its description—*evergreen.* Green means life. It means growth and fertility. And green is surprisingly responsive to encouragement. Deserts respond to rains with carpets of grass and flowers.

But I have to ask myself, *Is my soul responsive to the rejuvenating rains of God in my life? Do I give myself time to soak in that refreshing presence, or am I constantly on the move, dodging the showers of grace because more and more demands and urgencies present themselves?*

No wonder our spirits are rest-*less!* Where are those tranquil moments, those holy spaces for contemplation, for spiritual renewal and insight, which the Christian mystics spoke and wrote about with such spiritual fervor?

We live in a world (and I'm thinking particularly of Western culture) which seems to be accelerating at a frightening pace. Just keeping up with the technology, learning to use the new (and expensive) tools, useful though they may be for communication and research, can be a time-consuming, even an all-consuming, enterprise. The brand-new computer I am writing on right now, with its built-in programs and the latest software and hardware, will, no doubt about it, be obsolete in two or three years. I may spend hours a day writing and receiving e-mail messages, and "keeping in touch" with friends and colleagues, but am I really able to communicate with them heart-to-heart, in the quietness and privacy of waiting before God together? Do you, like me, find it almost impossible to pray with friends online? Praying on the phone is something I am often called to do, in moments when a friend is in crisis or anguish. But nothing can take the place of spending hours in communion with God and close prayer partners. Even the silences are filled with divine Presence.

Finding uninterrupted time with friends of the heart—time when we can enter holy space with God—is essential for the kind of deep, searching human relationships we crave as believers. We might call these "Trinitarian friendships," because beyond the friend-on-friend intimacy, they embrace that vital third dimension of intimacy with God.

But what about time apart from friends, time *alone?* I am not a born contemplative. Waiting in God's presence has often felt like a difficult discipline for me. As a mother of five, I have enjoyed a multi-track life and have had to balance family, prayer, worship, teaching, studying, writing, business, and recreation (re- creation!). Being alone became for me a vital part of spiritual and emotional health. Without some seclusion I might have gone crazy! But solitude is different from loneliness, because often loneliness is not a choice, whereas we may *choose* solitude. And that choice involves some serious planning. It doesn't often happen naturally.

My favorite way to be alone is to find a place of unspoiled wilderness, to set up my tent and sleeping bag and spend a week alone sleeping, reading, praying, meditating, and eating simple food. In my journal I keep track of my thinking and decisions made in that time alone. And my life is refreshed by it.

I believe Sally has a vital message about Sabbath rest for all of us. She has reminded me of things I knew already but still need to learn. Perhaps, as you live through these pages, you can learn along with me.

—LUCI SHAW
Bellingham, Washington
February 2002

Acknowledgments

M<small>Y MOTHER AND FATHER TAUGHT ME TO LISTEN TO PEOPLE AS</small> they talked about their lives. "Everybody's story would make a best-seller if written by the right person," they used to say. They were right. *Thank you.*

My husband believed in me long before I believed in myself. *Thank you.*

My children, Kent and Melissa; Ellen, Jon, and Brittany; Steven; Millie; and Thomas, give me my best opportunity for wonder and for reality. *Thank you.*

Jennifer Ennis prayed, Paula Rinehart opened a door, Beth Pendergrass stood beside me, and Marajen Denman sat with me over countless cups of coffee to make sense of a messy manuscript. *Thank you.*

Nanci McAlister welcomed me into NavPress with uncommon graciousness. My editor, Karen Lee-Thorp, helped me to speak my heart better than I could have communicated it on my own. *Thank you.*

And my women friends—you are the best. You told me your stories with honest hearts, and in your lives I see the face of God. *Thank you.*

Soli Deo Gloria

IN THE DEEP SOUTH, WHERE I WAS BORN, PEOPLE WOULD TALK, like people do, about the things they wished would happen. Many of those things they knew would never come true. So they'd sigh, then add these words to the end of their longings: "But it'll never happen in a month of Sundays." That's a long time—thirty of them, in fact. But why Sundays? Why not Mondays? Sundays used to represent holy, different days. You could go to church and sing "This Is My Father's World" and believe it was true. You could come home to the smell of roast cooking and anticipate a whole afternoon of talking and being with family. You didn't have to do anything, be anywhere. It was a good day. A month of Sundays strung together would be close to paradise, and close to impossible. Could we ever have a heart like that, a heart that lives like it's always Sunday? If we did, it would have to be a garden heart set in the midst of a city life.

A Garden,
a Longing, a Gate

For all of us the story began in a garden, a shimmering jewel cradled within an unblemished creation. In that place beauty abounded and life flowed in rhythms of work and rest, intimate connection and God-filled solitude.

We know the story. The two who lived there risked it all to obtain the one thing withheld from their reach, and in that winning they lost. They began to die. As God drove them away, the hope of ever returning to that garden vanished forever. Divorced from the source of life, expatriated from their home, they were left to face their work, their relationship with each other, and their solitude away from the garden, away from God, their Creator. In the rigorous monotony of cultivating the very soil from which they were taken, they would encounter their own dying. To prevent their ever returning to that first home, God stationed majestic heavenly creatures and a spinning, flaming sword to block the way back. On that day paradise was truly lost. Every generation since then has known that something is wrong. Longings and restlessness, sorrow and death find their way into even the best places of our existence.

But the story does not end in tragedy. From before the beginning, God has planned restoration. We have His promise. Those who know Him are headed toward another garden, far removed in time from that first one. This second garden exists within the protection of a great walled city. Large enough to encompass all God's own, the city is exquisite, bejeweled, ever lit by the glory of God. At its center is this new garden, built along the banks of a river that flows straight from the throne of God. Park-like and simple, it is a perfect balance to the lavish beauty of the city. Fed by living water from the very throne of God, the trees within that garden bear fruit with patterned faithfulness. Full healing abounds there. In that place all that was taken from Adam and Eve will be restored, and all that was put upon them as they left that first garden will be removed.

In the meantime, however, we live in this in-between place, feeling much of what that exiled first couple felt. Our bones grow weary; life is hard and dull. Longings gnaw at our souls. Our work rarely works out easily; frustration and exhaustion are its likely companions. Quiet evenings where God comes calling and we linger with Him in conversation must only be the stuff dreams are made of. Married love seldom flowers into that intimacy where two people lose their souls to each other, becoming more deeply themselves in the process. Most every relationship in this in-between place speaks more of incompleteness than it does of joy. For the present we live with aching, frustrated hearts, swinging pendulum-like between times of frenzied accomplishing and brain-dead relaxing. We live in the grip of our fears, our lists, our loneliness, our compulsions.

God understands. The story of Jesus' walk on this planet reveals that what we feel in this in-between place pierced His heart as well. But God more than understands. He is passionate to heal us. He yearns for us to be free to set our sights on that future city-garden and to one day live there. His longing is so great that He died for all the sinful brokenness we have brought upon ourselves, each other, this world. His death and resurrection broke the power of the dying that began in the first garden. Now He has gone ahead to make ready our place in that gardened city.

As wonderful as God's desire for us is, the question of this in-between place still begs to be answered. How do we live now? Are we resigned to existing without a heart, without a garden? Are we left with defining the meaning of life by the sweat of our brow? Can we expect nothing more than the frustrations of our own mortality at every juncture of our lives? No. The Scriptures invite us to learn to live a city life (full of people and labor) from a heart nurtured in a garden. They invite us to learn rest. The invitation isn't just for heaven, but for now.

We are a tired and weary people, and yet the Scriptures call us to live from expansive, expectant hearts that know rest at their core. But we have so misunderstood this rest that we may not know what we are longing for. Rest is not numbing or dead-ening our hearts so they no longer bother us. Rest is not some idealized place where we solve every issue and satisfy every long-ing. What is it? Rest is that garden place, the place created for Adam and Eve, the place where every Christ-follower is headed. We recognize true rest in people of faith around us. It flows from their hearts even as they experience the turbulence and weari-ness of life in this world.

The Bible says we have the opportunity to enter that garden rest even in this life. But for our souls to receive it, they must be made ready. As we tend and cultivate our hearts, God will forge space within our souls. In the process, we will realize that our longings and our issues, our dreariness, our heartache, and our heaviness do not have to block our entrance into that garden. In fact, God intends for these very things to become the gates by which we enter His place of rest. My own journey to that garden rest began in a very unexpected way. Let me explain.

It happened twenty years ago, but the impact of her words lives on. Maggie and I were chatting together outside, watching her two children and my two older ones ride their Big Wheels down our driveway to the grass of the back yard. We were friends as well as neighbors; from my front door, I could look through the yard across the street and see her back door. Because of the connection that had developed between our husbands, their family joined our church and a small group that met every Sunday night in our home. Our preschoolers played together almost daily, and she attended a neighborhood Bible study I led. It was early spring; the longer days and warmer weather stretched out before us as a token of what lay ahead—late-afternoon play for children, summer suppers together, swimming at a nearby pool.

But the conversation took a turn I never would have anticipated. "I don't want to be in your Bible study anymore," Maggie blurted out. "I'm so tired of all your questions. You want to know everything about me, but not because it's me. It's like you're gathering information to stack your life up against. You have no rest inside you. By the time I leave the study, I'm just worn out from you."

Her words shocked me, but the accuracy of her accusation pierced a deep place within me. I apologized and asked her to change her mind. But she was adamant. It was the end of the Bible study and the end of our relationship as far as she was concerned. In the next months I floundered. Perhaps she was just mad and would get past it, but all my efforts to revisit the issue failed. Her little girls no longer appeared at my front door. I struggled as I told my children again and again that we probably should not invite their family over to play.

As a cool politeness settled over what had once been friendship, quick solutions looked tempting: turn to friends we had in common and ask them what they thought about what she had said; find someone to justify me and write Maggie off. In my mind I argued with her indictment. As a young mother, young wife, young Christian, how could I see life as anything but an endless series of tasks to be executed as flawlessly as possible? I recognized that I struggled with issues of control and fear in some relationships, but it seemed that everybody I knew had similar battles. Yet no matter how I thought it through, I could not escape the power and weight of her words.

Her indictment paralyzed me by naming something I knew was in my soul, knew was eating me alive—something I didn't know how to cure. I had a restless, restless heart; it was not a place to be at peace, to be at home. On the contrary, my heart was a place of such constant disarray, hurry, and fear that there was hardly room for me inside it. Much less Jesus.

Even as I faced the reality that I could not repair the friendship, longing for a deeper healing came into focus. Ten years before this encounter with Maggie, I had trusted God to save me through His Son Jesus Christ. Sometime after that, I found Jesus' promise, "Come to me, all you who are weary and burdened, and I will give you rest. Take my yoke upon you and learn from me, for I am gentle and humble in heart, and you will find rest for your souls" (Matthew 11:28-29). Seeing my life through Maggie's eyes, I realized I was far from experiencing that reality. Too embarrassed to ask anyone around me for help, I turned instead to the Bible. What did God have to say about rest? Several phrases from Hebrews 4 came alive, exposing me and calling me to follow:

> Therefore, since the promise of entering his rest still stands, let us be careful that none of you be found to have fallen short of it. . . . It still remains that some will enter that rest. . . . There remains, then, a Sabbath-rest for the people of God. . . . Let us, therefore, make every effort to enter that rest. (verses 1,6,9,11)

Both the promise and the warning of these words blazed to life. God had made available a reality called rest, yet it was possible for us to fall short of it, to miss it. Furthermore, although God named this gift *rest*, it was something we were to make every effort to enter. I was confused: What kind of effort? How would a person work hard at not working? The words that followed gave a clue.

> For the word of God is living and active. Sharper than any double-edged sword, it penetrates even to dividing soul and spirit, joints and marrow; it judges the thought and attitudes of the heart. (Hebrews 4:12)

Evidently, as God's Word exposed and penetrated my soul, I would find His rest. His Word would explain me to myself and heal the things that kept my heart so restless. It would show me what it meant to "make every effort" to enter that rest.

THE COMPANY OF RESTLESS PEOPLE

You too may long for a still and full heart. You question if it's possible to make it through life's turbulence without being jarred and whipped around by every change in the weather of your world. Fatigue from the constant turmoil of pressures, worries, and unmet desires weighs heavily on your soul. Then added to those things may be issues that seem insurmountable: grief that cannot find an ending place, deep places of hurt, depression that won't lift. Whether your struggle is mundane or profound, you hunger for something that will quiet and refresh your heart.

Christine knows the longing for contentment and a rich sense of well-being, and she doesn't like remembering all the dead-end roads she's taken to try to get there. She learned the Christian pattern of endless activity early and well. As a teenager she used annual mission trips as opportunities to excel as a leader. When her heart said there had to be more than wall-to-wall action, travel, and being in charge, she decided to try marriage. Choosing quickly, she chose poorly. As her marriage spiraled down into a volatile coexistence, she began the gargantuan task of overhauling her husband and controlling her children.

Fifteen years later, having made little progress toward either goal, she turned to work, a place with adult people and tangible rewards for competence. By skill and good connections, she landed a job at a fast-moving start-up company. The company soared and so did she, at least on the outside. Disappointed that success couldn't fill her heart, however, she began to dull it with alcohol and frequent shopping events. But nothing eased her restlessness. When her marriage fell apart, the divorce only fueled the fire of her search. Maybe a new city, a new job, maybe work in a Christian organization would fill her aching core. She's still at it, going from one thing to the next, but the peace she seeks is like a highway water mirage on a hot summer day; as soon as she comes close to reaching a new goal, it vanishes again.

Other women experience the restlessness of their hearts in more subtle ways. Ruth just aches. Outsiders see her as a strong, successful single woman, but she knows differently. Despite her professional training and recent promotion, she will never have the place in her dad's eyes that her brother does. For starters, she's female, and from her father's perspective, that means she doesn't really count. Second, her father and brother are both surgeons, while she is "just" an engineer. She fills her life with good things: acting in the community theater, volunteering as the graphics person for a charitable organization, caring for her dog, who keeps her from dying in the silence of her empty townhouse.

These things help, but the low-grade heart pain never goes away. She doesn't fit. She cannot relate to her single friends who obsess about marriage. Neither can she completely enter into the world of her married friends. Sooner or later, she runs into an invisible wall. She tells herself she ought to value her professional training and her independence, but the emptiness of not belonging to someone and the meaninglessness of not having someone who needs her gnaw at her soul. A few months ago she sent me a copy of a prayer from her journal. The prayer contained this sentence: "I am so lonely, dear God, what will ever fill up my heart?"

For Emily it's been a drop over the edge of an abyss. Will she ever find peace again? She had known for months that something was wrong, deep down, with her fifteen-year-old son. No words came when she tried to verbalize what she sensed, but she was scared. Coaxing him to open up or resorting to the interrogating questions parents ask when they are desperate had yielded nothing. Then one afternoon as she put his clean laundry in his room, she felt an overpowering urge to open his closet and look inside the shoeboxes where he kept his baseball card collection. Never having been a snooper, she resisted. But before she could walk out, she found herself at the closet door. In the third box she discovered what she'd intuitively dreaded: drug paraphernalia, pictures, CDs that made her guts wrench.

Her husband was in the midst of one of the most critical workweeks of his life. How could she distract him with this? But how could she carry it alone? Even if they both knew, and even if their son recovered from the breach of his privacy, and even if he were willing to work on his issues, even then, healing would take a long time. Return voyages to sanity and wholeness are never instantaneous. How could she possibly have a heart that lived at rest in the midst of it all?

Hearts that do not know rest are not just a modern phenomenon. Almost since Creation, our hearts have been restless. At the serpent's enticement, Eve became restless for more than the garden offered. As God removed Adam and Eve from that place of beauty, they passed to us a restlessness that settled into the core of our being. Deep, deep down we hunger for what was lost. Instinctively we long to find some perfect place. The stories in Scripture confirm that restlessness is the built-in condition of being human.

Abraham and Sarah struggled to find peace without children. The children of Israel grumbled for forty years in the wilderness; nothing met their desires and expectations. King David prowled the balcony of his palace with a heart restless for some new pleasure, some new thrill. King Solomon accumulated wife after wife. The writer of Ecclesiastes despaired that anything could satisfy his soul.

The New Testament reveals this same inner *dis*-ease. For years the woman at the well in John 4 searched for someone, anyone who would just love her. Judas was restless for something more than just being Jesus' follower and friend. Until the Crucifixion, Peter had an unquenchable need to be head man of the inner circle. Before his encounter with Jesus, Paul saw life as a series of opportunities to prove his superiority.

In fact, the honest testimony of people throughout history confirms the truth of our tossed-about hearts. St. Augustine, a North African of the fourth and fifth century, probed the world through intellectual genius and sensuality, but nothing captivated and filled his soul. Moving to Milan brought him in contact with the great preacher Ambrose, but his struggle only deepened as he listened to this man speak the same gospel his own mother, Monica, had taught and lived. The ache in his heart was immense, and the Scriptures appeared childish; he saw no way God could bring him the freedom and fullness he craved. In His mercy, God used Ambrose, Monica's lifelong prayers, and ironically, the words of a little girl at play in the next-door garden to draw this man to salvation. His masterpiece *The Confessions* reveals our heart as well as his own. He sums up the reality found at the core of every person:

> You arouse [man] to take joy in praising you, for you have made us for yourself, and our heart is restless until it rests in you.[1]

Similarly, several Christians who lived in sixteenth-century Spain understood that our basic trouble is heart trouble. A peasant whose family had been forced to convert from Judaism during the Inquisition chose the name John of the Cross when he learned firsthand the love of God. Together with Teresa of Avila, a Spanish Carmelite nun, he spoke passionately about the heart of God and the need for revival in the human heart. Opposition from the church thundered against him. At one point his opponents locked him for six months in a broom closet where he was unable to stand. After his escape, he fluctuated between being heard and embraced by the church and suffering renewed attacks, beatings, and imprisonments. But his enemies could not suffocate his passion. Knowing the presence of God, he spoke and wrote about it until his death. His work *The Living Flame of Love* speaks of how the soul is meant to "cross over from its own empty silence into an expectant quiet that is alive with His presence."[2] That is rest of heart.

SEEKING A REST THAT LASTS

You may well know what an uneasy heart feels like, and you have probably sought your own methods for coping with the restlessness. You have heard the persistent inner voices, just as I have, telling you that all is not really well with your soul. In the process you have probably pursued ways to find your own way back to that garden rest. You may have chased desire after desire. Perhaps you've moved from one set of friends and activities to the next, believing that just around the next corner you would find something to fill up the aching places, the bored places. A man commented about his wife recently, "I've paid for her to go back to school, given her the capital to start her own business, lived through a period where the whole house was engulfed in her unfinished art projects. Now she's on to becoming a massage therapist. But it won't last; nothing ever does with her."

I sympathize with that woman, for although my neighbor Maggie exposed a true problem in my life, her words did not lead me to a quick cure. For a significant number of years after that, I continued to find life exhausting and frustrating. An incident seven years later revealed to me how far I was from rest. Roaring down the highway with my five children in the car, on my way to accomplish one more thing, I flipped on the radio and heard a radio preacher yell out, "Serve the Lord with gladness!" Usually I am immune to shouting radio preachers, but this time the words cut to my soul. My heart's immediate response jolted me out of the rushing and planning and doing that dominated every day. I didn't serve the Lord with gladness; I served Him with *madness*. I was so tired of all I had to do. For more than several years I had been on a mission to understand rest. Evidently I still had far to go.

During those years between Maggie and the radio preacher, I employed several different tactics to find rest. You may have tried some of these very Christian-looking dead ends to forge a heart of rest for yourself. Perhaps you will see yourself in some of my efforts.

I tried to make sure I had my theology right and to make sure I really believed. Truth is the great beginning point, but it never produced what I was looking for: a heart really at peace.

I worked hard at obeying everything I understood from Scripture; but a nagging, underlying layer of self-doubt still troubled my soul. Had I really done it right, really done enough? At times I exhausted myself, but I could never shake the reality that no matter how much I did, there were always good things left undone, things that shamed me and caused me to feel guilty, telling me I did not yet deserve rest of heart. The conclusion grew clearer with time. Earning rest by obedience is similar to the endless treadmill of running a home. We women know there is always one more job that could be done. Furthermore, when obedience became my goal, I became preoccupied with cross-examining my progress by looking at the people around me. The only way to know how I was doing was to make sure that I was doing a little better than the next person. The game of comparison has no ending, no rest.

I tried to "let go and let God." At first glance this seemed to promise hope for a life of rest. But I have never figured out exactly what it means. Obviously, it doesn't mean I give up all work. God has never sent a crew of angels to take care of my house or my budget or my phone calls. Rarely does God whisk my worries away. He often *does* work out the particulars of my schedule, taking days that seem overwhelming and making them sane when I ask for His help. Sometimes His peace does fall gently into my heart like quiet snow on a winter afternoon. Yet I know I can't just throw up my hands and expect Him to do my life for me. Although the concept of letting go and letting God makes some sense emotionally and spiritually, how to do it usually eludes me.

I made a concerted effort to live by spiritual disciplines. Cultivating a life of prayer, solitude, fasting, reflection, denial, service, and praise has refreshed me in ways I never before experienced. But although the disciplines make my spirit stronger, they are not enough. Deep inside of me I need the reality of the presence of God. I need a garden place in my soul, a place from which to live. The circumstances and the people of my life and the inner dialogue of my own heart speak with such intensity that they often muffle the voice of God. I have lived long enough to know I will never get all these things under control. *I need a way for the very things that seem to keep me from rest to become the gate to rest of heart.*

WHAT IS THIS REST, ANYWAY?

From God's point of view, rest is not an accessory blessing. Our lives are meant to flow from a solid garden core of spacious inner quiet. When we turn to the Creation story we see how foundational rest is.

By the seventh day God had finished the work he had been doing; so on the seventh day he rested from all his work. And God blessed the seventh day and made it holy, because [on the seventh day] he rested from all [his] work. (Genesis 2:2-3)

Take a Break

What does it mean for God to rest? The Hebrew language has more than one word for rest; this one, *shabath*, means to cease or desist. The most basic meaning of *shabath* is "to stop." Although God had finished creation, He was not removing Himself from active involvement with our world. For example, we know from Psalm 139 that He hovers over the formation of every unborn child. The picture throughout Scripture is that He actively participates in and directs the affairs of man. He speaks; He intervenes in the flow of events; He orchestrates outcomes far beyond our ability to produce. Furthermore, although Genesis 2 informs us that God rested on the seventh day, we know that an even greater work lay ahead: securing our salvation through the incarnation, death, and resurrection of His Son. In purely human terms, the *rest* of Genesis 2 means "to take a break."

Celebrate

The sense of taking a break dovetails with a second meaning for rest. *Shabath* also means "to celebrate." God took time off from His work in this world to have a party, to sit back and admire what He had created. Was God speaking to this truth when He asked Job, "Where were you when I laid the earth's foundation? . . . On what were its footings set, or who laid its cornerstone — while all the morning stars sang together and all the angels shouted for joy?" (Job 38:4,6-7). Evidently Creation took place before a watching party of angels who joined God in celebration once the work was finished.

SUFFER TO BE LACKING

Creation called for a party, and parties mean we take a break from work. But we know from our own experience that many things are left undone even as we choose to stop and celebrate. Another angle on *shabath* will help us here. Rest also means "to suffer to be lacking." God was certainly aware that much more work lay ahead of Him in this world even as He finished creating it. He has continued to be aware of that reality throughout human history. It is meant to be the same with us; when we see that all work is not finished, for a period of time we suffer, or allow, things to remain lacking. Often our greatest struggle with rest arises from this quarter. For example, we long to help our child with more of her college expenses, but we simply can't. The hard place we are in financially means we can only step aside and let her work the situation out. Or we realize as our fortieth birthday fades into the past that we will never be pregnant and give birth. How do we rest when things that seem so essential are lacking? We find rest in the incompleteness of the present moment as we learn to rec-ognize the goodness of what is and as we trust that what is needed for the future will be added at the proper time.

If we are to know rest at all in this life, it will have to be like this—a time when we stop; a time when we celebrate what is, in all its goodness and blessing; a time when we suffer or allow some things to still be lacking. At its core, to rest is to give thanks for the present and to trust that, as the future becomes the present, God will supply what we need.

A SETTLED HOME

A second word for rest in the Hebrew, *menuchah*, can give us fur-ther clues. Psalm 95 remembers the years the children of Israel wasted in the wilderness: "For forty years I was angry with that generation; I said, 'They are a people whose hearts go astray, and they have not known my ways.' So I declared . . . in my anger, 'They shall never enter my rest'" (Psalm 95:10-11).

The word that is used for *rest* in this psalm is *menuchah*. It means "abode, a settled home, a place to be." The Hebrews used this word to talk about marriage. Naomi says to her daughter-in-law Ruth, "Should I not try to find a home [that is, a rest] for you, where you will be well provided for?" (Ruth 3:1). Rest is more than ceasing, more than celebrating, more than learning to live with incompleteness. We find rest as we enter into a true relationship with God. Though we do not always have the words to express it, our hearts long for the rest of intimate connection and faithful, covenant love.

SABBATH

If Christians understand and attempt to rest at all, it is often only in the context of observing the Sabbath, a particular day of the week. But the concept of rest did not originate with the fourth commandment, "Remember the Sabbath day by keeping it holy" (Exodus 20:8). It goes much deeper than the commandment. God wove the principle of rest into the very fabric of creation.

Before the Law was given to Moses, in the instructions for the Passover in Exodus, God commanded His people to observe a seven-day abstinence from all leavening in their diet. Holy days of feasting, convocation, and resting preceded and concluded this week like bookends, reflecting the reality of a rest built into creation.

Similarly, once the children of Israel escaped from Egypt, God's method of providing food for His people highlighted the necessity of rest. Promising He would double His provision on day six, God gave no manna on the seventh day. These days were holy ones for Sabbath or resting: "He [Moses] said to them, 'This is what the LORD commanded: "Tomorrow is to be a day of rest, a holy Sabbath to the LORD. So bake what you want to bake and boil what you want to boil. Save whatever is left and keep it until morning"'" (Exodus 16:23).

The people's response to this command reveals how deeply our hearts struggle against rest. Despite the bounty of day six, the morning of the seventh day found some Israelites attempting to gather food in the dawn-light. Like many of us, they were determined to stockpile provisions, believing that rest could only follow a sense of visible security.

Even before rest became a part of the Law, God wanted His people to learn to stop, to celebrate, to trust that tomorrow would work out even if they took the breaks He prescribed. He longed for His people to be at home with Him, to realize they needed time when relationship, not work, filled their souls. When He finally gave Moses the commandment that the Sabbath day was to be a holy day, God's intention remained the same. He wanted to bless and enrich His people.

Moving to the New Testament, we see Jesus clarifying what Sabbath means. He broke the legalistic guidelines the Jews had established for Sabbath-keeping, but He did not break the Sabbath. Instead He redirected it toward its original purpose. He healed a lame man so the man could arise and carry the pallet that had been his prison. He walked with His friends through fields ripe with grain, plucking and tasting the goodness of fresh wheat warmed by the summer sun. He celebrated the Sabbath by using it for what God intended, the blessing of man.

In our own day we intermingle and confuse the ideas of Sabbath and rest. Christians have taken every imaginable stance toward the Old Testament concept of Sabbath. Some have chosen legalism and rigidity, a far cry from rest. Others have rightly called us to a true sort of Sabbath-keeping, a deliberate setting aside of time for renewal, rest, and relationship. The dialogue between Christians concerning the Sabbath can be confusing and divisive. But in the midst of that discussion, we often overlook what is most precious. God Himself is calling us to enter His rest and to live our lives out of a free and quiet heart. Hebrews 4 urges us to make every effort to enter into a life, not of Sabbath-keeping, but of Sabbath-living.

Here is our challenge: God has a gift for us, a gift that flows from the very life He enjoys. That gift is rest. A rest that frees us from the cycle of endless doing and allows us to take a break. A rest that invites us to join in celebrating all that is good and beautiful. A rest that assures us that everything is really going to be all right, even though everything (from our perspective) is not yet taken care of. A rest that eases our loneliness and allows us to find a true home in God.

But we have a problem, a great hindrance that keeps us from the rest we long for. We assume that we will only find rest when we solve all the issues that disturb our hearts. Some of our struggles are small in the grand scheme of things. Will our proposal be accepted at work? Will we ever make real friends in the new city we've moved to? What will we do with our difficult in-laws when they arrive for their annual five-day visit? But these small things can still eat away at the rest of heart that Jesus has promised.

On the other hand, some of our issues feel cosmic in their dimensions. Our grief for our stillborn child is a river of pain within us. Our marriage cannot be repaired. Our health is gone for good. Life for years has seemed utterly meaningless, and we cannot convince ourselves otherwise. Whether our issues are too small to bother our friends with or so huge they engulf us, we will never put to bed all that concerns us in this life. But God, in His creative turn-about way, intends that the things that keep our hearts in turmoil become the very gates through which we enter into that garden place that was lost at Creation. Spaciousness of heart, a depth of stillness that embraces both solitude and intimacy, and sheer joy wait for us on the other side of those gates.

Do you long for all that distresses you to become the very gate through which you can find rest of heart? Read on. In the next six chapters we will examine some of the core issues that keep our hearts from rest. Chapter 2 speaks of the havoc we let other people bring into our souls. Chapter 3 deals with that vague sense of uneasiness that hovers inside us, the disquieting voice that says there must be more to life than this. Chapter 4 addresses contentment—we will never know deep rest unless we believe that, in spite of it all, our hearts are really full. Chapter 5 tackles our fears. Do we have to solve every one of our worries before our hearts can quiet down? Chapter 6 speaks to the raw places of our deepest griefs. Can a heart filled with tears and a heart at rest coexist? Chapter 7 takes us to that very alone place that some people call "the dark night of the soul." When the trap door opens and we fall into the murky depths of our own heart, when the darkness around us seems impenetrable, God still has ways to meet us in the blackness and give us His rest.

You may be at such a place in your life that you would be better served by first reading the chapter that speaks to the issue that keeps your soul in turmoil. Feel free to do just that. Then you can come back and read the other chapters with a quieter heart.

Whether you read chapters 2 through 7 in order or not, be sure you read chapter 8. It's not just soul turbulence that keeps us from the rest of God; so before we are finished, we'll need to take one last long and honest look at our culture and at ourselves. The world we live in operates at a pace that can kill us all. To learn rest, we will have to learn how to resist the endless demands our world places on us. Furthermore, our hearts are strangers to rest because we are frankly afraid to be still, to be quiet, to be alone. We have to deal with our frenetic culture and we have to face our heart's stubborn resistance to rest; we'll do just that in chapter 8.

But let's begin with the things we are more easily aware of, the issues that disturb our peace. Often that's where we first notice that our souls are worn out; that's where we realize how deeply we long for the very thing we so seldom find—rest of heart.

Taking Time

1. *If my soul were truly at rest . . .* Finish this sentence for yourself by imagining what it would be like for your own heart to be
   at rest. I would feel totally at
   peace, esp. about my writing work.
   I wouldn't get all hobbly in my
   heart. I would reap the rewards of
   a quiet heart. ♥

2. What strategies have you developed to find rest for yourself?
   Have you succeeded? What have you learned from your efforts?
   Journaling, buying more books,
   joining exercise programs + bible studies,
   breaking to have myself to my
   publisher, numbering out on the
   computer

3. Consider the picture the Bible paints of a life lived out of
   Sabbath rest. Imagine, in the context of your own life, what it
   would mean to stop, to celebrate, to allow yourself to suffer
   lack, and to find a true home for your heart.
   I think this is what I've
   been looking for. ♥

4. Pick one area where you are willing for biblical truth about rest
   to begin to shape your perspective and choices. What is that
   area? In connection with the part of your life you have chosen,
   what are you being called to believe and to do?
   Writing — called to turn it
   over and trust God —
   to not quit

2

THIS PEOPLED PLACE

WE CHOSE QUIET FOR NEW YEAR'S EVE IN 2001. AFTER ALL THE uproar surrounding the new millennium, we were ready for something much smaller. Our married children were with their other families; our college son, away at a Christmas conference; a daughter, at a dance; the youngest one, spending the night with a friend. With all seven of those we loved dearest accounted for, we planned to enjoy dinner and the last night of sitting by the Christmas tree with good friends. As my husband sat with the men by the living-room fire, the other wives helped me in the kitchen with last-minute dinner preparations. When these friends asked about one of our children, I gave a brief sketch of the progress I saw this child making, then added, "I really do feel at peace, but there is still a knot in my stomach."

Both of the other women laughed. Then one responded, "I don't even know how many years I've lived with a knot in my stomach about one or another of my children." Our joint laughter mellowed into mutual empathy. Confession feels good when others join us in it. Both of the women in my kitchen that night are God-loving, God-believing women. I enjoy their friendship because they strengthen my sense of confidence in the goodness of God. They are women who seek to live out of rest of heart, but they too know the knot in the stomach.

People. They really do have a way of disturbing or even wrecking our heart rest. At times they seem to expect so much from us; to our distress we can't change them; and often we are hard pressed to really forgive them. Every one of us is well aware that the people in our lives can send our hearts into tumult. In fact it often seems that the state of our very soul is tied to the ebb and flow of our relationships. We know what we long for: a deep inward stability that will empower us to love with an open heart and to endure through the difficult times—the rest of living well even while some things are incomplete or lacking in our relationships. We wish we knew the secret of being able to delight in our relationships without having our lives made or destroyed by people—the rest of being able to celebrate the goodness of what is. We look at Jesus; He lived so engaged and yet so free. He did not experience life as a knot-in-the-stomach existence, even though He cared passionately about the people around Him. How do we learn that sort of rest in the midst of difficult relationships?

If we examine where our disquiet in relationships comes from, we can pinpoint at least three issues that destroy the rest of soul we long for. First, our heart rest crumbles under the strain of what we think other people expect from us. Second, our peace is often attached to the well-being and behavior of the people we love. Finally, when we carry the weight of all we are unable to forgive, our hearts stagger under the load of remembered hurts. And we have no rest.

EXPECTATIONS: STRUGGLING UNDER THE WEIGHT OF IT ALL

How do we find rest of heart in the midst of people who expect so much from us? The pressure of too many demands from too many people is an enormous issue, fueled to fever pitch by the endless possibilities for relationship and responsibility that fill our world. Do we acknowledge every e-mail? Participate in every neighborhood association event? Respond to every plea when they ask for volunteers? Meet with every person who asks us for time? Send a birthday card to every friend? Obviously the circumstances of our day have heightened the number of choices and seemingly obligatory events available to us; but generations of people have struggled with the demandingness of life.

Last fall, as we toured the Smithsonian exhibition on the First Ladies of the United States, I was struck by a quote from the correspondence of Louisa Catherine Adams, the wife of the sixth president of the United States. Perhaps her statement was the result of the heavy responsibility that rested upon the wives of prominent men to make numerous social calls to the wives of other important men. The records show that at one point, this First Lady made sixty calls in four days, an amazing feat accomplished by carriage transportation and without the availability of the telephone to set up appointments. Louisa Adams wrote, "The more I bear, the more is expected. I sink in the efforts I make to answer such expectations."

Mrs. Adams was not a weak woman. Raised in Europe, the daughter of a prominent couple, married to a man who loved her dearly, surrounded by servants whose job was to make her life easier, she had every advantage imaginable to make her life work. But at times her world, like ours, seemed overwhelming.

Life hasn't changed much. A few years ago I met regularly with a group of women. One of the women had a lot to say. She had chosen to be self-employed, hoping that would give her flexibility to manage her home, orchestrate the scheduling involved in life with three daughters, and keep the financial books for her husband's business. Into that mix she had added a volunteer job: the chair position for a community theater group. Every time we got together, she was frazzled.

The conversation ran for weeks along the same track. Over and over she said stress is just part of life, as if saying it enough would make it better. She also said she enjoyed her life. But as she reflected within the safety of our group, I wondered if she enjoyed *anything*.

One evening as we met together, her life, and my own, came into sharp focus. She told us how her middle daughter had said to her little sister, who innocently brought the message back to her mother, that she wished their mom wasn't always on the phone, that her paperwork wasn't all over the kitchen table, that meals weren't always fast (or eaten in the car on the way to the next thing). But even as she related the story, this woman did not seem to be moved at all by her daughter's longings. Life was just the way it was.

Then a younger woman, with more courage than I had, spoke up. "Shouldn't you listen to your daughter?" she queried. "I think she is trying to tell you something." Once again this woman dismissed the incident. Life demanded so much and she was doing her level best to give it. As I watched the flow of the conversation, questions tumbled inside my head. How could she stand the pace? Why couldn't she hear her daughter's heart? Didn't she realize how she came across? She seemed so unapproachable, so caught up in all the people and projects of her life.

But just as quickly, my thoughts headed in another direction. I remembered snatches of conversation that people have directed at me: *You seem so busy; I hate to bother you. . . . I can't imagine you would have time, but if you do, I would love to talk to you. . . . Don't you ever stop?* I wondered, *Am I like this woman?* If she couldn't recognize it, even when her daughter begged for quiet, for less, if she couldn't reflect on her life even in the safe context of a group of friends, then what was I blind to in myself?

That small group no longer meets, but I still need to ask, just as many of you need to ask, *Do the demands of all the people and projects in my life wind my heart into frenzy? Do they lead me to lay aside any pursuit of heart rest until I get just one more thing done? Am I like this friend, yet can't see it either because the haste and pressure of my life have created such a blur?* Many of us know firsthand how the push of people and responsibilities destroys our ability to do what God did as He finished His creation. He stopped; He took a break; He rested. We sometimes think we simply don't have that luxury. Can we learn to live differently? Several scenes from Jesus' life give us insight.

FOCUS ON THE HEART OF THE MATTER

> Someone in the crowd said to [Jesus], "Teacher, tell my brother to divide the inheritance with me."
>
> Jesus replied, "Man, who appointed me a judge or an arbiter between you?" (Luke 12:13-14)

Jesus knew the pressure of people's demands. We often see other people trying to draw Him in to settle their arguments: Tell my brother to divide the inheritance with me. . . . Tell my sister to help me. . . . Tell us which one of us is the greatest. In these potential conflicts, we see Jesus establishing priorities rather than directly solving the issue: Be rich toward God. . . . Realize only a few things are important, really only one. . . . Choose the place of the servant. He simply declared the truth of the matters at hand and then lived by them personally. That meant He was willing to live in the midst of relationships that were far from perfect; He was willing for the present moment to be lacking.

We cannot sort out or solve every issue in life. We cannot stop the frenzy of our culture nor satisfy everybody's expectations. But we can affirm what matters to the heart of God and then determine to live by those things for ourselves. If we are going to learn to live out of a heart at rest, we will have to learn to leave things undone. In that process, we will find the gate to a spacious rest, space in our lives for the presence of God—for what matters to Him—and space for each other.

TURN TO THE ONE WHO CAN HELP

Many of us live stressed out because we are convinced that it's all up to us. If we don't do it, it won't get done (at least not in the way we'd call right or best). Scripture records two different times when Jesus knew there wasn't a place or a means to buy food to feed the huge crowds of people that had gathered to hear His teaching. He questioned the disciples for their suggestions, but they had no answers. Jesus did the only thing that was left. He prayed. God answered by providing supper.

Similarly, Jesus looked ahead and saw the temptation that Simon Peter would face the night of His betrayal. Knowing He would not be physically present to help Peter, He told Peter that He would pray for him. He did, and although Peter failed, he made the turnaround back to true faith: "Simon, Simon, Satan has asked to sift you as wheat. But I have prayed for you, Simon, that your faith may not fail" (Luke 22:31-32).

If we are going to live out of a heart at rest, we must make the fundamental faith decision that no matter how deep or urgent the need is, it is ultimately not all up to us. We must choose to believe that God is at work in small things, in underground things, in unseen things, in not-yet-known things. As we rest in this foundational reality, the stress of what we cannot handle becomes a gate to rest.

BE PRESENT TO THE PRESENT MOMENT

One of the most amazing revelations from the biographies of Jesus' life is to realize how fully He lived His life from the moment at hand. In the inauguration message of His ministry, the Sermon on the Mount, Jesus calls us from our worries to life in the present. By pointing to the Father's care for His creation, Jesus illustrates how we are to receive life, His own living conveyed the same message. He looked ahead, knowing He would be betrayed, knowing He had the anguish of the Crucifixion to undergo, knowing people from other times and cultures would come to faith in Him. And yet as we read His encounters with individuals, we see a man totally present to the present moment. A hemorrhaging woman caught His full attention; so did a widow dropping her coin in the offertory box. He dealt with arguing disciples and a demon-possessed boy, even though their troubles came swift on the heels of the glory-filled moments at the Mount of Transfiguration. The present moment absorbed Him.

If our minds race to all that needs to be done, if they plan and scheme and worry, if they never learn to just be present to the present, we may miss God; we will miss the people of the present moment; and we will most assuredly lose out on rest of heart.

WORRY: WILL THE PEOPLE IN MY LIFE DO WELL AND DO RIGHT?

It's not just people's demands that pull our hearts from rest. When we attach the well-being of our souls to the behavior and attitudes of those we love, the knot-in-the-stomach syndrome is inevitable. Worrying about the people we love means we will miss living from a still heart at almost every turn.

Amanda is trying to learn a life of rest. She's so weary of having her peace of heart chained to how her husband and daughter are doing. Her husband is a good man. Part of the unrest she feels comes from feeling so guilty because she is not satisfied with him. She longs for her husband to have a true spiritual hunger. She wishes she could talk to him about all the things she thinks about. She frets because he doesn't take more leadership with the kids. Even though she hates herself every time she does it, she prods him to do more than just dutifully show up at church and sit beside her. She's never doubted his faithfulness, his ability to provide well for them. He takes their two boys camping and listens when she worries about Jill, their seventeen-year-old daughter. The way Jill dresses, the friends she's choosing, her new closed-off personality have Amanda scared to death. So Amanda's heart frets, tossed about by longings and troubled by guilt. She tells herself she ought to be more trusting toward Jill and more grateful for the husband she does have. Where does heart rest come from when we live with imperfect relationships?

PLACE OUR HOPE

As we face our worries over the people we love, we must first decide where we are going to place our hope. Part of maturity is watching the diminishment of the number of things we hope for. Most young women have so many hopes: hopes about what we will accomplish, the kind of man we will marry, the children we will have, the people they will grow up to be, the way our friendships will develop. But the years disappoint many such hopes.

I am a blessed woman; some of my dreams have come true. But it is also a very real fact that many of them have not come true at all. I have known real pain because of people. Family, children, and myriad relationships in almost thirty years of pastoring churches have taught me that I will get hurt; I will be disappointed. So what happens when our hopes are crushed? What happens when we live with ongoing tension in the relationships that are precious to us?

Life is precarious. God is true, His Word is true, but there are very few outcomes we can count on. You know those fears and hurts. You have wondered about the same things that make all women anxious at times: *Will my husband be able to pull out of the depression he's in, or will I forever live with a defeated man? Will my mother-in-law ever accept me, or will I sense for the rest of our relationship that no matter what I do, I won't measure up? Will I ever find someone to love me? Will my child ever give up her self-destructive choices? Will my beautiful thirty-five-year-old daughter ever find a husband? How will my child make it in this world with the handicaps he has?* It goes on and on, so where can we put our hope?

> Not only so, but we also rejoice in our suffering, because we know that sufferings produce perseverance; perseverance, character; and character, hope. And hope does not disappoint us, because God has poured out his love into our hearts by the Holy Spirit, whom he has given us. (Romans 5:3-5)

We miss out on rest of heart because we think we must have guaranteed answers. But in those times when anxious thoughts multiply within our souls, we have the opportunity to place our hope in the truest things. We hope to become women who rest, celebrate, and love well even in the midst of adversity. We hope to know God's tender presence even when people most disappoint us. Ultimately, we hope for the day when we will see God face to face and all tears will be wiped away.

COUNT ON HIS LOVE

According to Paul, the hard things in our life give us opportunities to keep doing the right thing, and as we keep doing the right thing, we begin to learn what really matters. The thing that really matters, the only thing that can be counted on, is God and His love for us. We will never find rest of heart if we expect all our hopes and dreams for the people we love to come true. But if we let the hard things in life whittle us down to the essentials, we will discover the love of God. As we learn to make our home in His love, His rest will flow to us and from us, for His love never disappoints.

After I finished a teaching time with a group of women a few months ago, a woman a little older than I am came up to me. She had been weeping throughout the Bible study, and she needed to talk. In almost litany fashion she began pouring out her story to me: for years she has lived in distress over a prodigal daughter . . . she still can't understand where her daughter's rebellion came from . . . she was the oldest of four, adored by her younger sisters, doted on by her father and grandparents. This woman was living as many of us do, her emotions swinging between believing God would answer her prayers and obsessively thinking about her eldest daughter. Whenever her thoughts turned to this child, her heart constricted into a small and anxious place.

That morning in the Bible study, she heard me say what I have just written here, that ultimately there is nothing we can count on in this life but the love of God. But this woman was afraid. To choose the love of God sounded like stepping into an abyss. I understand. When we let go of our anxiety, when we let go of our demanding prayers, we think we are losing our last place of influence. We are afraid that if we don't stay tied to that person with at least a small thread of worry, then we, and they, will free fall into darkness.

But what is our choice, really? I have wasted hours being tense about damaged friendships, worried about conflict in churches we have pastored, hurt over misunderstandings with my husband, fretting about my children, rehearsing my disappointments with extended family. And to what end? Ultimately, we can make only two choices about the people we love, but those two choices give us the freedom of a spacious and peace-filled heart. We can learn to do the right thing when relationships are hard—that's persevering. Then, as that perseverance transforms our character, we discover what's ultimately important in life. With that new perspective we can make the second good choice, the choice of hoping in the truest things. The truest thing of all is the love of God, and it will never disappoint us. As we make these choices, we find the gate to rest of heart in the midst of our worries about the people we love.

FORGIVENESS: THE ONLY WAY NOT TO CARRY ANOTHER'S SIN

Many times, the biggest reason why the people in our lives cause us such unrest is that we cannot forgive them. We load ourselves down with grudges, remembered hurts, and unsolved issues, and our hearts grow weary under the load. Some people can forgive easily. I am married to one. I had one for a mother. Quick forgivers. I envy them. Because I am still struggling with learning to forgive, I am glad that Jesus told Peter to forgive his brother seventy-seven times (Matthew 18:21-22). I need the exhortation to keep re-forgiving and the comfort of knowing that Jesus understands how short-lived my forgiveness can be. Rather than shaming me for not being able to hold on to a forgiving spirit, He simply tells me to forgive the same offense or the same offender again and again.

Rest means we celebrate the goodness of what is, but when we hold onto grudges, mentally rehearsing all that had been done to us, we become blind and deaf to the goodness around us. We never find the gate to rest. To learn forgiveness we need truth from God's Word to help dig up the root of bitterness that so easily grows in our soul. If you find your soul wearied by all the grudges you carry, the following insights from God's Word will encourage you to be a person who practices mercy. Only as we learn to forgive will we enter God's good place of rest.

MERCY TRIUMPHS

God says in James 2:13 that mercy triumphs over judgment. If personal justice is our primary concern, we will never be able to forgive. Consider what took place at the cross. In God's eyes we all stood justly condemned, but in His mercy, He sent His Son to take our condemnation. Justice was satisfied at the cross, but mercy triumphed. As we deal with people, we may be right in our "judgment" of them or their actions, but we can still choose, like Jesus, to let mercy triumph and to forgive them.

Realizing that mercy triumphs over judgment brings to mind the old adage "Everybody wants justice done, except for when it comes to their own life." It's true. We want justice in situations, and we want other people to act justly and receive just consequences when they don't. But in our honest moments we know that for ourselves we don't want justice done; we want mercy. We need to turn the table on ourselves. The same mercy we want, others want as well.

WHATEVER YOU BIND WILL BE BOUND

Jesus' words in Matthew 18:18 are puzzling: "I tell you the truth, whatever you bind on earth will be bound in heaven, and whatever you loose on earth will be loosed in heaven." Perhaps they are an encouragement to forgive. If we release someone from our hearts by forgiving them, if we refuse to bind them to us with cords of grudges and bitterness, then perhaps the freedom in heaven that Jesus talks about will be the freedom God has to begin working in that person's life. On the other hand, if we bind people up by not forgiving them, then perhaps God hesitates to begin a work of conviction and change in their lives. Is God asking us to give up our grudges because they limit His freedom to work in the other person's life? If so, the best way for me to hasten change in that person is to let go of my issues with them.

PAGANS AND TAX COLLECTORS

Robert Capon, in his book *Parables of Grace*, takes a fresh approach to the last part of Matthew 18:17: " . . . and if he refuses to listen even to the church, treat him as you would a pagan or tax collector." According to Capon, we have to wonder what Jesus really meant in telling us to treat unrepentant people like pagans and tax collectors. Did Jesus mean the way Jews treated pagans and tax collectors or the way He treated them? It's quite a question. Jesus absolutely denounced the religious leaders who lived in pride and hypocrisy and misled others; but

He was always hospitable toward sinners. So perhaps the call in Matthew 18 is to treat sinful people with grace and hospitality. If so, we cannot claim that we want to be like Jesus and continue to hold on to our judging and begrudging spirits.

CONTAGIOUS DEFILEMENT

Our forgiving is never a private heart issue. Hebrews 12 has a strong warning for us: "See to it . . . that no bitter root grows up to cause trouble and defile many"(verse 15). Can you think of one person you know who has a soul infested with grudges and yet has been able to keep her feelings within her own heart? Like toxic waste, unforgiveness leaks out. It's contagious, polluting. Whole families are separated by it.

I have friends who live on the same street with their first cousins. Both families are Christians; both go to churches. But the mothers, who are sisters, had a disagreement a number of years ago that they won't let go of. They stopped speaking. Now each family has isolated itself from the other. Each husband took up his wife's stance. The children bought into it, too. All of them showed up for the grandmother's funeral, still refusing to reconcile. We can say that our lack of forgiveness would never be that extreme, but the same truth applies to every one of us. If our spirits are bitter, they will defile. We have to ask ourselves, are our grudges worth the cost?

BLASÉ ABOUT GRACE

Finally, when we don't forgive, we don't understand the nature of our own forgiven-ness. Forgiveness is costly, but it is never paid for by the one being forgiven. We know that because of the Cross. We have missed the point when we feel like we can't forgive until the other person does something first (says she is sorry, makes restitution, tells me what a wonderful person I have been to endure her behavior). God forgave each one of us without asking for anything. That is grace. If we require something from the one who has wronged us before we can forgive them, we don't understand grace. Releasing another person this completely is usually beyond our ability. If it is for you, realize that the God of grace forgave you before you did anything to earn it. The more His grace astounds you, the more it will compel you to be like Him and just forgive.

∽∾∾

Grudge carrying is wearying to the soul. It keeps our hearts in a constant state of disruption. It blinds us to God's work in the present. We go over and over the past; we imagine confrontations where we will set the score right; we wait eagerly for future tidbits of the other person's continued wrongdoing. We are far from love and far from rest when our hearts carry bitterness.

I know the necessity of forgiving all too well, yet sometimes the ability to forgive eludes me. A number of years ago I found myself struggling to forgive a man who had deeply hurt my husband's ministry. At the time we lived in a neighborhood where several of the streets joined in a figure-eight pattern. Almost daily as I went for a walk, I struggled with the issues I had with this man. Around and around that figure-eight route I would pace; and around and around my heart would go, twisting back on itself as I remembered injustices, dreamed of vindication, and imagined this man confessing to us and others how wrong he had been. But nothing changed. The man continued to do his damage, and I continued to damage my own heart with what I could not forgive. Gradually, I began to use the insights I have just written about to speak truth to my own heart, and gradually, I began to release this man to God. As I learned to forgive, the gate opened to a spacious place, a place uncluttered by the hurt and injustices of the past.

From my perspective, that was the end of it. Five years later we received a letter from this man. In His own time God had convicted him, and he was writing to ask our forgiveness. As I read and reread that letter, astonishment was my primary emotion. I realized I no longer needed his confession and apology. The work that God had done in me had gone to the core of who I was. Long before his letter arrived, God had freed my heart from what he had done. Forgiving depended only on the reality of my heart connection with God.

Whether we live lonely lives or ones overflowing with relationships, people cause us heart turbulence. We feel the weight of all their expectations and, if we are honest, the weight of all the expectations we impose upon ourselves for what we think we must do for them. But the pile of all we could do will never be cleared away. The gate to rest opens when we are able to enjoy the goodness of a relationship in the present moment. Can we learn to rest our own souls, rest our relationships in the goodness of God, or do we believe that everything we do has to reach a certain level of perfection?

It's true with our worries as well. We can fret forever about the people we love, always on the lookout for a way to improve or protect them. Or we can find our rest of heart in the home of God's love. When we are rooted in rest, we can weather our worries because we see a far bigger picture than the immediate situation.

Weightier, perhaps, than either of these issues is our inability to forgive. When we don't forgive, we have no rest. It's that simple. In our very struggle to give in to forgiving, we face the bitterness of our own souls. In that place we have one of our finest opportunities to learn the love of God for the other person, and ultimately for ourselves. As God's mercy touches our broken and resistant hearts, we forgive and let go, and in that releasing we find rest.

Taking Time

1. What is it about other people that most destroys your own rest of heart today? The stress they cause? The worries they provoke? The wrong things they do? How could dealing well with these very issues become a gate to lead your heart to rest?

2. What would it look like in your life if you were like Jesus, deeply engaged in relationships, yet truly free from expectations, worry, and bitterness?

3. What would it feel like to have a spacious heart, one that you could open to others?

4. What will be today's step toward rest in your relationships?

THE LAND OF
SHADOWS

IN OUR MOST HONEST MOMENTS, MANY OF US KNOW THAT WE cannot blame our lack of rest on the people around us. Objectively, life may be going well, but an underlying motif of disquiet still runs through our days. Before we open our eyes in the morning or clear thoughts form in our heads, our hearts ache with a vague sense of trouble. The empty grayness of our interior life moves within us like a fog. As far as we can tell, life is hollow at its core.

In the past few years, Nancy has felt the tug of the emptiness and the shadows. Before that, she had always believed that rest must lie just on the other side of the next challenge, and she has had a few. Her husband left when she was thirty years old. With two children to support and no education to fall back on, those first few years were an exhausting struggle. Then wonder of wonders, she married a man who had plenty, who enjoyed making more, and who seemed happy for her to enjoy his success. When they had one more child, she worked hard to blend the children into one family. She even cared for Randy's mother in the years before she died and with far greater enthusiasm than her mother-in-law's own daughters did.

Twenty years have gone by. Her husband continues to be an incredible producer. In fact, he works harder than Nancy likes. She wishes he'd slow down. She's done everything she knows to fill in the gap while she waits for him. She spent a small fortune remodeling and redecorating their home. (Randy said the cost didn't matter; he trusted her.) She planned and executed the weddings for her two older daughters, joined a book club for her mind, a gym for her body, the church Bible study for her soul, and a birthday luncheon club in hopes of finding a real friend. But it all keeps getting more and more empty.

The house seems huge and expensive and over-appointed with pretty things; both the girls live in distant towns, so her visits with them are far apart. Her third child is fifteen, with little interest in her mother; and Randy is still Randy, out of the house by 6 A.M. to hit the gym so he can get an early start on a long day of deal-making and meetings. Two or three times a year they take a nice vacation together, but the stretch from one of these times to the next looms before Nancy like an empty, hollow metal tunnel.

Does God understand when our heart aches and we can't figure out why? Nancy feels so guilty about the hurting vacuum inside. She has everything a woman could want, it seems, and yet she still isn't satisfied. If Nancy could talk to her fifteen-year-old daughter, Kaitlyn, she would discover that Kaitlyn sees her own life stretching before her with that same hollow weariness. She too aches with guilt for feeling this way. She has two parents who give her so much that other girls have to work for—a nice allowance, a closet full of clothes and CDs, the prospect of a car as soon as she turns sixteen. She's been to summer camp in the mountains every year since she was eight. She's taken tennis lessons, ballet lessons, horseback-riding lessons. She's been with her family on amazing vacations. When it's time for college, her dad will pay; and when it's time for her wedding, she knows it will be just like her sisters'—beautiful. But every morning as Kaitlyn's alarm goes off, the same question fills her heart: *What's it for, anyway?*

The predominant cultural answer for the ache Nancy and Kaitlyn feel is an antidepressant, the traditional folk remedy is "get busy," and the Christian response is often "be thankful and serve." All of these suggestions are well meant, and all can help, but sometimes when our heart aches with emptiness, we need something more. We need to listen, for in paying attention to the shadows that push against our soul, we will find a profound gate to true heart rest.

The Ache Is Our Gift

Years ago one of my then-high-school-aged children was struggling with the seeming emptiness of all things. I tried all the traditional encouragement: "Think of what you have to look forward to; think of how blessed you are; think of how much we love you; think of how much God loves you; try being thankful." Finally, in a moment when all my answers were failing, I said to this child, "Why don't you go read Ecclesiastes? God understands; maybe it would be good to see that."

A couple of hours later, he reappeared in the kitchen as I was making supper. "Well, what did you think?" I asked, as I noticed that he had his Bible in his hand with a finger holding it open near the middle.

"Mom," he said. "That's exactly how I feel." A look of relief hovered in his eyes, brightening his face for the first time in days.

There will be no gate to rest in the midst of the shadows of life unless we first face what we feel. That means we have to take time; we go for a walk to think rather than to get exercise. We turn off the music in the car. We sit on the swing on our back porch, by ourselves. We listen to what our hearts say to us. We find in the process that God is not afraid of the ache in our heart.

In fact, God gave us the gift of Ecclesiastes to expose and record the gray emptiness of life on this planet. Item by item, the writer of this book examines the stuff life is made of, then declares that he has found nothing substantial enough to give life meaning. Pleasure, accomplishments, possessions leave the heart empty even when we achieve a full measure of them. Work for work's sake is unsatisfying, and no matter what our work produces, the instability of circumstances and the passing of time destroy what we have done. Furthermore, despite how productive we may be, work rarely produces the satisfaction we thought it would. All people, regardless of their circumstances, experience the pain of lonely living. Righteousness cannot provide reliable protection from the folly and evil of life. Money seems all-important, but it buys so little. Death appears to destroy all hope of meaning.

Ecclesiastes is a virtual catalog of what will not work to bleach the shadows out of life. The writer comes to his conclusion several times, but he sums up what he feels in this statement: "So I hated life, because the work that is done under the sun was grievous to me. All of it is meaningless, a chasing after the wind" (Ecclesiastes 2:17).

It is important not to rush over his ache, or the ache of our own soul, by moving too quickly to the answers Ecclesiastes gives. We need time to feel and to ponder the issues of life; authentic faith is not a methodology for bypassing the difficulties our hearts face. Several years ago for a whole springtime I sat in a Bible study with a group of women who never seemed to feel the shadows the way I do. As far as I could tell, everything was always fine with all of them, and God was always wonderful. I wondered as I gathered with them week by week but never really got to know them, *Where does all their pain go?* Haven't they ever felt the ache? I still don't know the answer to that question, but I do know from the Bible itself that deeply believing (which I do) and feeling the ache are sometimes the warp and woof of our existence. They are woven together in a way we cannot separate. Only as we admit the ache to ourselves and to God can He respond to the shadows in our soul with truth that will heal us.

For as we embrace our ache, letting it speak to us, we will hear the voice of God; He alone can turn our gloom into a gateway to rest. As we sit with our aching souls in shadow lands, the teacher of Ecclesiastes speaks.

> I have seen the burden God has laid on men. He has made everything beautiful in its time. He has also set eternity in the hearts of men; yet they cannot fathom what God has done from beginning to end. (Ecclesiastes 3:10-11)

God has burdened us; in truth, He has put us in a bind. On this planet, we experience gray emptiness of heart. But we also sense the beauty of life, and as we do, our heart responds in a way that overflows our soul. Yet even in those deepest joys, we still feel the ache.

I remember the hours following the birth of our second child, our first daughter. I had taken the abundance of males on both sides of our family as an indication that we would never have a daughter. Beyond that, after our first son was born, it appeared that we might not be able to have another child. After a miscarriage, a struggle with fertility, and a difficult pregnancy, a healthy baby had finally arrived—and arrived in female form. I was overwhelmed with wonder, overwhelmed with love, overwhelmed with the beauty I saw on that small round face.

Several hours after delivery, my husband left to get our son so he could meet his new sister. Alone in the hospital room, I began to cry from the goodness of it all. God had given overflowing blessing, and my heart's response was the ache of beauty and gladness. My daughter was lovely; she had safely joined our family. About that time, a nurse roared into the room with juice and a thermometer. Seeing my tears, she stopped short. "Is everything okay?" she asked. (I could imagine all the possibilities for tears that were going through her mind.)

"Yes," I said, "I'm just so happy."

Her expression softened; her brisk, efficient orientation dissolved. "I know," she said, "tears of joy." Why does joy have that ability to create such a deep ache that our response is tears? Why do we cry when we see courage and love united in an act of great self-sacrifice on a movie screen? Why does the loveliness of a summer morning, or the upturned face of our child as we say bedtime prayers with him, or the Rocky Mountains etched against the evening sky cause our hearts to hurt?

The writer of Ecclesiastes understood. God made us to respond to the beauty of the moment, yet He also made us for eternity. We ache because as the moment touches us, we realize we cannot hold onto it. We ache because we sense in a way we cannot express that all moments are meant to fit into some grander scheme of things. We know, deep down, that beauty like this cannot be the result of random collections of molecules.

Ultimately, I believe we ache because we are caught in cross currents. Beauty is so lovely and yet so ephemeral. Pain is so predictable and raises such unanswerable questions. Daily life is so often tedious and small. We were made for something. We are sure of that, but that something eludes us. The beauty of the present moment pierces us through, then quickly slips from our hand. Our hearts want much—they can be deeply touched—but though they are touched, it never lasts; it is never enough. We carry the burden of eternity in our hearts. Still, it is meant to be a good burden, a burden that will carry us to the heart of God. The very longing, like the drab grayness of the shadows, is a gift to open the gate to rest.

THE PRESENT IS OUR JOY

Then I realized that it is good and proper for a man to eat and drink, and to find satisfaction in his toilsome labor under the sun during the few days of life God has given him—for this is his lot. Moreover, when God gives any man wealth and possessions, and enables him to enjoy them, to accept his lot and be happy in his work—this is a gift of God. (Ecclesiastes 5:18-19)

Just as the ache of life gives us opportunity to touch on what is eternal, so the present moment is the temporal place most connected to God Himself. To each of us, God gives the present as a gift. The goodness of *right now* is not a complete answer to the shadows, but it is a true answer. Our relationships, our work, our food, the unfolding of the seasons—these gifts from God's hand are meant to touch us, to slow us down. So often we think that God's highest requirement on us in the present moment is thankfulness. God does call us to thankfulness, but He holds open a door to much more than that. He calls us to live with a sense of wonder, even mystery, as we let the present speak to our souls.

Our culture fights powerfully against such an orientation; as Westerners and moderns, we are goal focused, future oriented. Every company, organization, and church that wants to stay on the cutting edge is constantly retooling its mission statement. But purpose statements never fully answer the *why* questions that stir inside our hearts. Why *are* we planning such a huge, expensive party for our husband's fortieth? Why did we take on the chairmanship of the landscape committee for our subdivision? Why did we set (or allow others to set) such impossible goals for our job? Why have we decided that the really great church ministries are purpose driven rather than God oriented? When we seek to understand the purpose behind the purpose behind the purpose, it's rather like peeling layers off an onion. Ultimately, we find there really is no core, just layers. If we think we can get rid of the shadows by deciding the purpose for everything, we are deceived. The whys have no final answers here on Earth. We need to slow down our racing hearts. The Father above calls us to receive the present as His gift.

My children have taught me this more clearly than anyone else. Why did my sons spend hours a week on winter afternoons and evenings designing elaborate castles and space vehicles with their Legos? For no reason but the sheer joy of imagining and constructing. On summer mornings, why do I gather flowers from our garden and arrange them? Why do we spend holiday time cross-country skiing, or hiking, or camping? Why do we sit in our back yard on late spring evenings watching the gathering dusk give way to night? Instinctively, we know we truly live when we savor and relish the moment. As we choose wonder and enjoyment, we learn part of the melody line for rest.

At the end of time when all things are made new, when this creation is restored to the beauty that God first gave it, we will see that this ability to appreciate the everydayness of life is, at its core, an understanding of the fundamental holiness of the ordinary. As he looked ahead to the coming Day of the Lord, the prophet Zechariah said that "Holy to the Lord" would be inscribed on the bells of the horses, and every cooking pot in Jerusalem and Judah would be as holy as the sacred bowls in front of the altar. We lose the opportunity for rest of heart when we do not stand in awe of the ordinary, when we do not see that in the routine of life, from workhorses to mixing bowls, God longs to be present.

The generations that went before us had an intuitive ability to wonder at the everyday. For example, "In Chaucer's England one of the names for yeast or barm was goddisgoode 'because it cometh of the grete grace of God.'"[1] That mystery is still present in yeast. How can something so small, which floats spore-like and invisible in the air around it, interact with the sugar and gluten in flour so that the dough rises?

We do not know how or in what culture yeast was first discovered; the long stretch of history shrouds those beginnings. But as ages of women have gone about their kitchen work, have they given thanks as they watched the bread swell in the kneading bowl? Have they gently touched the smooth surface of the dough, aware on some level that yeast truly comes from the manifold grace of God?

If we are going to find the rest that comes from wonder, a rest deep enough to pierce the shadows with light and beauty, we have to take time. When we choose to be quiet, to listen in the midst of the daily-ness of life, the veil is sometimes drawn back so that we see in the ordinary the beautiful, holy presence of the living God.

I remember a Sunday afternoon like that. An African Christian leader and two other pastor friends had joined our family of seven for Sunday lunch. Several of the children had friends over as well, so a large group gathered around our dining-room table. The long, slanting rays of winter sunlight flooded through the windows. Geraniums bloomed red from a mass of clay pots. Classical music played in the background as we passed large pottery bowls of couscous and chicken, then of salad and bread around the long table. Despite the size of the group gathered, there was a quietness and tenderness in the air. It did not matter that Sundays were a long day of work for my husband and me. It did not matter that our hearts were heavy with concerns for one of our children and for our church. It did not matter that the food was simple, or even that the couscous had cooked too long and was gummy. The presence of God permeated the room, shone through the sunlight, and wove through the conversation and the passing of food. In moments like this, the question is not about purpose, it is about receptivity. In moments like this, the shadows of our heart move aside and we are at rest in quiet joy.

THE ENDING SHAPES THE NOW

The ache is our gift. The present is our joy. The writer of the book of Ecclesiastes has more wisdom; his next charge to us will further clear our vision, so that our hearts can find rest as we make our way through the shadows of life. He does not give us this encouragement, which is also a very real warning about life, until his book is almost finished. We can be thankful for that. This answer to the empty ache of life is not glib; it takes our angst and pain into account. His message, however, rings with certainty as he declares that our life and our choices really do matter.

> Now all has been heard; here is the conclusion of the matter: Fear God and keep his commandments, for this is the whole [duty] of man. For God will bring every deed into judgment, including every hidden thing, whether it is good or evil. (Ecclesiastes 12:13-14)

The writer makes no apology for his conclusion. He calls every one of us to acknowledge the presence and reality of the Holy God whose universe this is. He calls us to live with a trembling humility, discerning what pleases God and following through with full obedience. One day we will be exposed, and God will evaluate the real us.

Our first reaction to such an answer for the shadows that hover in our hearts may be that the writer is not helping us. We feel we need sympathy and patience. We object to the thought that God might require something from us before our hearts are fully healed. But the truth is the writer *has* let us feel; for twelve chapters he has let us struggle. Together with him and in every way possible, we have asked the question, *Does anything really matter?* Does it matter if you work hard? Does it matter if you're righteous? Does it matter if you are rich or poor? Does it matter how or when you die? He has felt it all, and in many ways he has not been able to answer his own questions. But the one thing the writer cannot escape is the absolute reality of the presence of God. There is a God. He is present. He is Creator; we are His creatures. One day we will give an account to Him. Our choices, our character, our ethics, our holiness will be held up against the plumb line of His perfect, holy righteousness.

When we let His words speak directly to our own soul, the ache in our heart is no longer the only thing we feel. We may be uncertain about the particulars of God's will, but one thing is clear: It matters how we live. This is God's universe, and He is rightfully the judge of all He has made.

The writer's conclusions are also clear: we are more than just our questions, more than just our ache. Ultimately we cannot hide behind those things. Beneath them all is a greater reality, the reality of our duty to God. As we understand that our choices matter and we act on that truth, rest of heart begins to break up the shadows that cloud our vision.

Agnes lives that reality; she is eighty-one, but the women at her church still come to her for advice, for comfort, for inspiration. Although she doesn't talk about her own story a lot, most of the younger women could sketch out her life from the bits and pieces she's told them in the Bible classes she's taught. She's buried one of her children, and a little grandchild. She and her husband spent thirty years doing missionary and agricultural work in India, working with the poorest of the poor. Agnes has stories to tell about living conditions that the younger women can't even conceive of, frightening stories of political unrest in the little villages where they lived. The women know one of her sons is divorced. They know she cared for her in-laws for the last ten years of their lives. They know her husband died fifteen years ago.

When the younger women begin swapping details of all they've learned about Agnes, they marvel. She has survived, triumphed really, in so many hard places. They know she is actually a very private person who at the same time has this incredible capacity to engage. Sheila, one of those younger women, asked Agnes once how she had lived through it all. She shared a simple phrase, a phrase found on the wall of an old manse house in England. The phrase goes like this, she told the younger women: *Do the next thing.* Do the next thing.

Surprisingly, that phrase is helping put Sheila's life into perspective. She's still struggling to accept the reality that she may be single her whole life. Three years ago her fiancé broke off their engagement, just six weeks before the wedding. She's thirty-five; her friends keep encouraging her that there's still lots of time, but it doesn't feel that way. She has plenty to do. That's not the problem, but she has also found that keeping busy is not the solution. Teaching school, coaching a girls' softball team, and volunteering at the food bank her church sponsors don't fill up the emptiness.

Sheila reminds herself of Agnes's phrase almost every day. Somehow those words are helping to break apart the shadows that have lodged inside her soul. Instead of hoping that her activities will act as a drug to keep her from feeling her loneliness, she is realizing that in them God is calling her to a life of faithful service and obedience. That's the point of the things she does. She can see the next thing that needs to be done. And she can take it on. One by one those next things done faithfully will pile up into a life well lived. Then one day God the Judge will examine all those next things. Sheila knows she wants His praise. She will do the next thing.

SEE THE LOVE

Our ache however is bigger than the answer Ecclesiastes gives. We arrive at places in our life where we can't see the holiness of the everyday, where the energy to do the next thing has been bled from our hearts, where we hardly care that one day we will stand before God the Judge. In those times the gray angst threatens to suffocate our soul, and the hope of rest of heart seems laughable. Without some sort of intervention, we doubt we will ever find a spacious and peace-filled heart. We need more, and God meets us in the shadows of our longings.

His final answer is the answer of love. But how do we move from simply affirming the correct theology that God loves us to an experience of that love? No matter how hard we try, we cannot simply rearrange our feelings, and even if we experience moments when the shadows break apart, a response to the truth that we are deeply loved by God is often a very elusive thing. Sometimes we feel loved; sometimes we don't. What can open up our hearts to the love of the Father?

I began to ask this question for myself ten years ago. I was sick to the point of boredom and frustration with the only form of Christianity I knew, the Christianity of correct belief and prompt obedience. Although I was definitely not a professional in terms of theology and my obedience record was pockmarked with failure, I had nevertheless lost my heart for simply improving in either arena. I struggled with how people made perfect doctrine the proof text for spirituality. As far as I could see, it led only to unending arguments and damaged relationships. I also knew obedience was often no true benchmark of spirituality. Because we had lived in divergent cultures across North America and had pastored enough different kinds of churches, I knew that a fair number of things that people held up as essential to Christian living had more to do with culture, preference, and legalism than they did with the holiness of God.

Please don't get me wrong. I appreciate the importance of understanding and communicating the truth. I respect the work of theologians, teachers, and preachers; without them we will not understand the beauty and depth of God's Word. I also believe God calls us to a thorough obedience so that we reflect the character of Christ in our attitudes, our decisions, and our lifestyle. But in the midst of a life of good theology and a will that wanted to choose consistent obedience, my soul still felt the shadows; it hurt with hunger for something.

God met me in that hunger. Conversations over coffee with friends, good books, long walks where I thought and prayed and watched the season change, difficult circumstances—these things began to shape new space inside my heart. Into that new space the Word of God came with a fresh clarity. I realized He was calling me into a heart relationship with Himself. He wanted to speak not just to my head, not just to my choices, but also to my heart. And the message He wanted to speak was love.

To help me understand that love, God began to show me something of the relationship that the Father, Son, and Spirit enjoy with each other. I had been a Christian for twenty-something years and I knew that the Trinitarian nature of God was an essential foundational truth of Christian doctrine, but I had never made the connection between the relationship they share with each other and our lives as people. As the time I spent in solitude and reflection began to open my eyes, I came to see that a beautiful bond of true affection, delight, and desire to bless flow unceasingly between the Father, Son, and Spirit.

For the very first time, I received insight into an astounding truth; these Three who are one God were drawing me to participate in the web of love they had been sharing with each other since eternity past. They did not send me blessing the way I might send a care package to a needy family. Neither did love begin when the human race was born. The love the Trinity shares—a love that is a place of rest, a place of celebration—has forever been real and full. The Triune God was inviting me to enter, to be a part of their love. The more I understood, the more I wanted the reality, not just the theology, of learning to live in the midst of that love.

Phrases began to come to life in the Scripture as I "overheard" the Father and the Son talking about each other and about the Spirit. Listen to what Jesus has to say as He talks about the Father and to the Father:

> The Father is the goal and purpose of my life. . . . Father,
> . . . Display the bright splendor of Your Son so the Son in
> turn may show your bright splendor. . . . Everything mine
> is yours, and yours mine. . . . You, Father, are in me and I

in you. . . . Father, I want those you gave me to be with me, right where I am, so they can see my glory, the splendor you gave me, having loved me long before there ever was a world. (John 14:28; 17:1,10,21,24, MSG)

Or listen as the Father speaks about His Son. Through the words of the prophet Isaiah, He says, "Here is my servant, whom I uphold, my chosen one in whom I delight" (Isaiah 42:1). At the baptism of Jesus, God proclaimed to the entire world from the heavens: "You are my Son, chosen and marked by my love, pride of my life" (Luke 3:22, MSG). The Father is so full of love for the Son that He broadcasted a similar message at Jesus' transfiguration: "This is My Son, the Chosen! Listen to him" (Luke 9:35, MSG).

When Jesus spoke of the Spirit, we see the same love: "I will talk to the Father, and he'll provide you another Friend so that you will always have someone with you. This Friend is the Spirit of Truth. . . . The Friend, the Holy Spirit whom the Father will send at my request, will make everything plain to you" (John 14:16,26, MSG).

Describing what happens in our souls as we hunger for that connection with God and then find ourselves drawn toward Him, the psalmist cried out, "Deep calls to deep" (Psalm 42:7). As we first become aware of the gray ache of life, we may think it is only the depth of our hunger for meaning that calls out to the unknown and murky universe we live in, but as we are drawn into God's love, we begin to realize that all along the Triune God has been speaking to the depths of our hearts from the rich depths of His love.

Is there a road map to that love? Not really. It's a journey from depth to depth. A journey each person makes alone. Some things are necessary: Time. Quiet. A willingness to learn to listen and to hear. And truth, the truth of God's Word, reaching into our hearts as well as our heads. As I began to examine God's love, four words came into focus that have shaped my understanding of what it means to be loved by the Triune God: *disciples, friends, family,* and *beloved.*

Disciples. In the book of John, the Lord Jesus calls us to be His disciples: "If you hold to my teaching, you are really my disciples. Then you will know the truth, and the truth will set you free" (John 8:31-32). This promise gives us a position of honor. Every great person has a circle of the privileged few who have the opportunity to be with him apart from the crowd, who get to know him and learn from him in an intimate setting. That door to His inner circle of followers, Jesus opens to us all. He is gracious, openhearted. No political or power system exists with Jesus, just a gracious invitation.

Friends. But then as His ministry draws to a close, Jesus makes the calling to relationship even more precious. At the last supper, Jesus changes the name He has for His followers; in John 15 He declares, "You are my friends if you do what I command . . . for everything that I learned from my Father I have made known to you." What a change of position for us! Great leaders have followers, but followers are different from friends. Friends are confidantes, people we enjoy, people we regard as peers. In every life a time arrives when most people leave, and just friends remain. In our home, when the door closes on good-byes after a big event, our heart friends often stay a little longer. We kick off our shoes, get comfortable on the sofa, and settle down for the "real talking."

Or perhaps a different image from our home will help. We have a living room where all sorts of gatherings take place—parties, meetings, Bible studies. But we also have a smaller room, sort of a library/office where we read and write and study. It's not really a room for guests, but there are those moments when our home is filled with people, and special friends come over with whom we want to have a quiet conversation. In those moments we go to our little study, pull up a couple of chairs, and talk as true friends. In the hours before His death, Jesus did not say that He was our friend; He said something even more startling—He said we were *His* friends.

Family. But that is still not all. In this journey of love, God draws us even closer. Go in your mind all the way to the garden of Christ's resurrection. Mary has encountered one she believes to be the gardener. When Jesus reveals to her that He is not the gardener but the risen Lord, He also gives her instructions about what she is to do with this Resurrection news: "Go instead to my brothers and tell them . . . " (John 20:17). *My brothers.* Once again He has elevated us, this time right into the heart of His family, gathering us within the love that flows so freely within the Trinity.

We have been loved this completely since time began. Part of Jesus' mission on this earth was to explain that the Father, the Son, and the Spirit have always had this heart toward us. We would never have known we were invited into the circle of their love if Jesus had not come. We work at being loved. We hide, we present, we manage our images, hoping that if we get it just right, people will be attracted to us. It goes all the way back to Adam and Eve and a closet full of fig-leaf clothes.

In contrast, watch Jesus. He keeps drawing us closer. *Disciple, friend, family.* The summary statement about this family connection comes in chapter 2 of Hebrews. This amazing Jesus, the writer of Hebrews said, is *not ashamed* to call us His brothers. Some of us have family members we are faintly or deeply ashamed of. We know there is no way to dissolve the connection we share, but we are most assuredly not going to be the ones to emphasize that we are related; embarrassment causes us to keep our distance. But the Son of Man, Jesus Himself, holds us up before all creation as His brothers. We do not embarrass Him.

Beloved. As the reality of that familial love began to settle into my heart, God took me to a new place. I was studying the Song of Songs for a class I planned to teach. I knew this book in the Bible had been interpreted as everything from a sex manual for married couples to a full-blown allegory of Christ's love for His church. How was I supposed to approach it?

One summer morning, I simply began reading it. I read it again and then again. It is definitely a romantic book. Its powerful imagery stirs up passion in a way that no modern book of tips and techniques ever could.

But the more I read, the more I heard another voice behind the voice of the young human bridegroom. That voice was the voice of Jesus, calling me to respond to His love, calling me not to be just His sister, but to share the sweetness of life as His beloved.

The Song of Songs is a prism through which the passionate love of our holy God shines, scattering that love abroad in all its splendor and beauty. In the shadow times of our lives, we ache for something that we often have trouble finding words for. We ache for someone to know us, to see all there is about us, and yet still delight in loving us, pursuing us, drawing us close. All through the Song of Songs, the bridegroom says, "Come close to me . . . let me see you . . . you're beautiful." The bridegroom delights in nearness, in intimacy. In our innermost core, all of us were made for receptivity, made for someone strong enough to hide us within His embrace. We all long, male and female alike, for someone to pursue us because He delights in us. In the midst of being loved like that, shadows begin to melt. Questions fade. Our hearts find rest because they find home.

The shadows will never fully disappear in this life. Yet by God's design, the gray emptiness is meant to open the gate to His garden of rest. We were made for so much, made to see the beauty and reality of Jesus through the lens of the everydayness of life, made for eternity and for the wonder of loving and being loved. We can cover up the angst, ignoring its call, or we can listen and let God lead us into a receptive, spacious place. In that place we will find a joy that plays among the shadows, a joy that finds the face of God. That is rest of heart.

Taking Time

1. Has there been a time in your life when the shadows were thick in your soul? What did you learn from that time?

Yes. This past month (Sept. '18) — I was frustrated by it. But it did lead me back to God.

2. If the ache in our hearts is meant to be a gift, sit with your ache for a few minutes today. Listen with your heart to what that ache is trying to tell you. Sit quietly. Think back through the twenty-four hours you have just lived. Where was the wonder of the everyday? What did you miss? Thank God for the beauty you now recognize.

I often miss the wonder in exchange for checking email, social. I want the wonder back.

3. It matters what we do. We will all give an account before a holy and just God. What do you think He longs to hear from you on that day?

4. Write out the words disciple, friend, family, beloved on a piece of paper. Put that paper where you will see it frequently throughout the day. Let Jesus Himself talk to you about His relationship with you.

4

THE GRUMBLE
GRINDS ON

*Hell . . . begins with a grumbling mood, and yourself
still distinct from it: perhaps criticizing it. And yourself, in a dark hour, may will that mood, embrace it.
You can repent and come out of it again. But there
may come a day when you can do that no longer.
Then there will be no you left to criticize the mood,
nor even enjoy it, but the grumble itself going on forever like a machine.*[1]

OCTOBER 23. TODAY IS MY GRANDMOTHER'S BIRTHDAY. IF SHE HAD
lived just three months longer, this day would have marked her
one hundred and second year. So much of everyday life still
brings her to mind. Although age and time reduced her flesh
to little more than a paper-thin, fragile container, her tri-
umphant and patient soul knew no prison. Then just six
months ago she walked into the very presence of the Father.

Today mirrors the real grandmother. Autumn is shouting
from every fiber of the landscape. Hickory trees stand like yellow
columns of fire among the pines. The sky is indigo blue, finally
free from the gauze of summer's humidity. She would have loved

[handwritten: I want to THANK God more than THINK / ANALYZE too much!]

today. In reality she knew the secret of embracing all days, for she knew contentment. But the gratitude and peace that dominated her spirit did not flow from a life where everything had worked out. By the end of her years, she knew as many broken pieces as she did realized dreams. Yet over time the fierce pain of her life served as little more than a dark backdrop to highlight the beauty of her soul.

The heartache started early, in a difficult marriage, with learning to maneuver her own and her children's lives through constant pressures and abuse. There she developed the wisdom and heart strength to ride the rapids of life, taking the crash-ups and hurts that came her way. From all she endured well into her sixties, old age should have provided a respite for her. Surely the God who had witnessed so much faithfulness from one slim, blue-eyed woman would see fit to reward her latter years with peace. But it wasn't to be. From age eighty-eight to ninety-nine, events continued with crescendos of pain. Three of her four children died in circumstances that had true elements of tragedy. Cancer attacked; her house burned down; she broke her hip twice. Life didn't let up.

The morning I heard that the third of her four children had died, she said something that revealed the essence of her heart. Calling as soon as I received the news of my uncle's death, I found her full of words: the love she had for this son, the beauty of God she saw in his life, her admiration for his desire to handle well the particular form of suffering that had come his way. I listened, glad for the deep connection we shared. As she came to the end of her thoughts, I broke in, trying to communicate how grateful I was to her for talking so freely. "Oh, Grandmama," I said, "It takes a lot of thinking to live life, doesn't it?"

Her reply was instantaneous: "No, Sally, it takes a lot of thankfulness."

I cannot recall what was said next or how our conversation ended. But in those few words, I saw the landscape of the soul that lives in the rest of contentment. *It takes a lot of thankfulness.*

[handwritten: A SOUL THAT LiVES IN THE REST OF CONTENTMENT → It takes a lot of thankfulness]

DISAPPOINTED, OR RICH OF HEART?

Like my grandmother, two remarkable men from the Old Testament, Moses and David, knew the fullness of a contented heart. They too had reason to express (or even to complain) what life had lacked for them, but they saw a far grander vista; each one saw goodness and blessing that dwarfed the difficulties their lives encountered.

MOSES: NOBODY'S HAD A LIFE LIKE OURS

Honest conversations with God punctuate the Bible's biography of Moses; he was not a man to hide his heart from God. One particular exchange near the end of his life speaks to this same reality that it takes a lot of thankfulness. As Moses' story comes to a close, God is beginning to give His people victory and territory on the east side of the Jordan River; but the event that Moses spent the last forty years of his life for, the crossing of the Jordan, had not yet happened. Moses knew God planned to deny him the opportunity to enter the Promised Land; an earlier sin had brought that sharp consequence (Numbers 20:12). But in the flush of these first victories, in the awareness that his life was nearing an end, Moses hoped that God would allow him entrance.

He had reason for hoping. From a human perspective, God appeared to change His plans when Abraham pled with Him to spare Lot in the destruction of Sodom and Gomorrah. Moreover, Moses had personal experiences of times when God seemingly altered His program. When he prayed for God to be merciful in the face of the rebellion and debauchery around the golden calf, God moved from a decision to destroy His people, to a decision to abandon them, to a pledge to continue to care for and lead them. Some months after the golden calf incident, God withheld another punishment He had initially decreed; He did not leave His people to their own devices when their fearful stubbornness sabotaged their entry into the Promised Land.

In view of all he knew of his Lord, we understand why Moses took the desire of his heart to God. His prayer cried out with longing to the One whom he knew to be good.

> O Sovereign LORD, you have begun to show your servant your greatness and your strong hand. For what god is there in heaven or on earth who can do the deeds and mighty works you do? Let me go over and see the good land beyond the Jordan—that fine hill country and Lebanon. (Deuteronomy 3:24-25)

God, however, responded with a fierce and direct answer: "That is enough. . . . Do not speak to me anymore about this matter." Did this second and very definite refusal from God stir up mutterings of discontent in Moses? Did he begin to see all he had done for God in a different light? Apparently not. In the very next chapter of Deuteronomy, we see a man filled with contentment, not bitterness or cynicism, as his life drew to an end. In recounting all God's blessing on His people and all He requires from them, Moses asked an amazing series of questions:

- What other nation is so great as to have their gods near them the way the Lord our God is near to us whenever we pray to Him?
- And what other nation is so great as to have such righteous decrees and laws . . . ?
- Has anything so great as this ever happened . . . ?
- Has any other people heard the voice of God speaking out of fire, as you have, and lived?
- Has any god ever tried to take for himself one nation out of another . . . ? (Deuteronomy 4:7-8,32-34)

Moses did not focus on what God denied him. He did not anguish over God's rejection of this last and very personal prayer.

As he related to the Israelites his amazing experience of shepherding God's people, his heart overflowed with a contagious contentment. *Nobody has ever had a life like ours.*

DAVID: FOR ALL MY DESIRE

King David gave the same testimony of personal contentment in the last song he wrote before he died. By family status and birth order, he was only an ordinary man, yet God anointed David and raised him to a high position. The song speaks of the inexplicable grace David experienced in being chosen by God; it also speaks of another great grace, the grace to receive whatever God gives as His best for us.

> Is not my house right with God? Has he not made with me an everlasting covenant, arranged and secured in every part? Will he not bring to fruition my salvation and grant me my every desire? (2 Samuel 23:5)

How could David say that God had met his every desire? Though David's life is a tale of the powerful goodness of God, it is also a litany of things that went wrong. Without doubt, his youth had its own set of sorrows. Growing up as the youngest in a family of seven sons, he was ridiculed and overlooked. His triumph over Goliath was short lived; he could easily have concluded that God let him waste the best years of his life as a fugitive from the raging jealousy of King Saul. In the personal realm, his wife Michal humiliated and betrayed him. Finally, his best friend, Jonathan, died when David was still a young man.

His maturing years brought a new wave of grief and disappointment. His adultery with Bathsheba and the death of their baby plagued his life. Years later, his son Amnon raped his daughter Tamar. Then another son, Absalom, retaliated by killing Amnon. Family chaos heightened as an embittered

Absalom instigated a rebellious coup, then disgraced David by publicly having sex with David's concubines. In the midst of that conflict, one of his most beloved counselors chose to betray him and join the opposition. Then, when David's men killed Absalom, his heart broke almost beyond remedy.

Even old age did not bring an end to his troubles. David made a humiliating and sinful choice, even as a mature and seasoned leader, to go against his own heart before God and against the advice of his most trusted advisor. In the discipline God brought into his life at that point, he had to watch his beloved nation suffer because of his own poor choices.

But beyond all these things, God denied David the very thing he most wanted: the privilege of building the temple where God would be worshiped. God not only declared that he could not have his desire, but God's grounds for that refusal were hard to accept. According to God, David had been a man of bloodshed, and God wanted a man of peace to be the builder. God's reasoning could have aroused immense frustration in David, for God Himself had charged this man with the responsibility to enlarge the territory Israel occupied. David spent his life carrying out God's plan, yet when it came to what David really longed for, God denied him the honor and joy of fashioning a building that would bring glory to God.

Yet as he lay dying, David declared that God's purposes and covenant had more than fulfilled the desires of his heart. Beyond that, as the door to eternity opened, David was convinced that he would only see the ever-growing goodness of God.

How many of us know this fullness of heart in the face of being denied the thing we most want? So often the story of our lives is a long tale of hurts and difficulties, regrets and unanswered questions, losses and unfulfilled prayers. Moses and David experienced all these things as well, yet they saw their lives through eyes ablaze with contentment. Moses challenges us: Ask yourselves. Look around! Nobody has ever had a life like ours! David sings it: God has given me all my salvation and all my desire.

Contentment. Without it there really is no rest. Yet our discontented hearts yearn unceasingly for something else, something more, something different from what we have. We are convinced life lies just around the next bend or in the acquisition of one more thing. We are sure contentment would flow into our souls if we could rearrange the past, removing the sting of old regrets. But in the midst of all that *isn't*, we can develop a soul that is truly at rest in what *is*. Recall that part of the definition of *rest* is "allow to suffer lack." God intends that our discontent become a gate by which we find our way to that spacious garden of heart rest. But first, we need to see what we are up against. Much of our nature fights against the gratitude that leads to contentment.

WHAT IS IT WE'RE UP AGAINST?

Our battle to learn contentment is often a fierce one. Some of our English words reveal to us how serious our problem is. Greed, envy, and covetousness are harsh terms, but they give shape to the vague feelings of restless dissatisfaction that ebb and flow within us.

The root for our English word *greed* is a deviation from the Greek word for grace. When our souls are swayed by greed, we misjudge the grace of God: We cannot see what we have as a grace gift from Him; and we choose to believe that what others have is a far better expression of God's goodness than the lot we've drawn. Little wonder then that Jesus said, "Watch out! Be on your guard against all kinds of greed; a man's life does not consist in the abundance of his possessions" (Luke 12:15).

Envy takes greed to a more destructive level. *Envy* is from a Latin root word that means "to look with malice." As we envy, we look maliciously on the people who have what we don't have. We no longer simply wish we had a different life. The spirit of discontent has poisoned our souls on a deeper level. We believe that what others have should be denied them until we've achieved a full quotient of happiness. Because Solomon saw the destructive power of envy, he warned, "A heart at peace gives life to the body, but envy rots the bones" (Proverbs 14:30).

Finally *covetousness* joins two Latin roots, one meaning "desire" and one meaning "vapor." These root words paint an accurate picture of the nature of covetousness. As coveting grips our hearts, we fritter away our lives in pursuit of things that only turn to vapor as we draw near. As James pointed out, even if our coveting becomes belligerent, it still leads to nothing: "You kill and covet, but you cannot have what you want" (James 4:2).

When greed, envy, and coveting rule our souls, contentment is far away. Our hearts are restless.

LEARNING BY PRACTICE

A third character from the Bible would understand our trouble. Contentment did not come naturally to him either. In fact, he said that he first became aware of his sinfulness when he realized he was a coveting man. This man was Paul.

By the testimony he gave in his letters, we know he spent his early life carefully keeping the Jewish Law. In terms of what his mouth said, what his body did, and where his feet went, he was without fault. But in his heart, that center place designed for intimate connection with God, he was a coveting, discontented, and restless man. In Romans 7 he makes this confession: "I would not have known what coveting really was if the law had not said, 'Do not covet.' But sin . . . produced in me every kind of covetous desire."

But after Paul's conversion, as his life became intertwined with and transformed by the life of Jesus, he was able to tell the church at Philippi that he had learned "the secret of being content in any and every situation" (Philippians 4:12).

Paul did not mean that life had brought him every pleasure possible. His biography, recorded in bits and pieces throughout the New Testament, makes that clear. Neither was Paul saying that he had learned to dull his longings and shrink his heart. Resignation is a false substitute for true spirituality. We will never become people who live out of contented hearts by cutting desire off at its source. Deadening our hearts and steeling our focus may discipline our minds, but it will never produce the spacious places in our hearts that true contentment does.

The conversations around us bear that out. I listened a few weeks ago as a heartbroken woman described how her daughter was destroying her marriage. This daughter had her husband in vice-grips with demands that he produce more and more income so she could buy more and more things. I have watched other friends shrink back from a mutual acquaintance whose intense longing for a friend makes friendship impossible. Recently in a small group, an honest and lovely woman confessed to all of us, "I don't know how to stop the discontent and coveting inside. There are things that go on in me that I can't tell anyone about, not my husband, not this group." A good marriage for your daughter, true friendships, peace deep inside. The answer to these mountains of unmet longings is not simply to learn to want less.

The Greek word for contentment that Paul used had a different meaning. It meant to have enough, to live from, a full heart. It spoke of completeness and strength, not resignation. Isn't this the rest we long for? We don't want our hands to go limp. We don't want to spend our lives telling ourselves that what we have is all we'll ever have, so we better learn to be thankful for it. We don't want to kill the deep desires, those longings for beauty and connection and purpose. Contentment must flow from a far deeper place in our hearts; then we will ride the current of our deepest desires, trusting that God is good and able to overflow our hearts.

THREE PERSPECTIVES OPEN THE GATE

Fortunately for us, in his letter to the Philippians, Paul did more than testify that he had learned how to be content; he also taught by his example how we can learn contentment for ourselves. Like my grandmother, he chose to embrace gratitude as he faced the difficult circumstances, the frustrating people, and the painful losses of his life. His perspective on these three things freed him from living in the prison of life's disappointments and flung open the gate to the rest of contentment.

THE STRESS OF CIRCUMSTANCES: A CHOICE TO SHOWCASE JESUS

In the first chapter of Philippians, Paul spoke frankly about his work as an evangelist and leader. His ministry had fallen on hard times. He was imprisoned, perhaps near death, and lonely. In the meantime, outside the guarded room that confined him, his opponents, jealous of Paul's place in God's work, were having a heyday, moving in on relationships and discrediting his ministry.

You probably know something of what he felt. You spend hours working on a committee. Your words are seeds that blossom into full-blown plans as the committee works. But no recognition comes to you. The aggressive, up-front people take possession of every idea and take credit as well.

You spend hours talking to a struggling friend, listening to her story again and again. Then someone else arrives in her life. You know you have given to this friend; more than that, you have grown to love her. But now she moves away from you, caught up in the magnetism of a new friendship, scarcely even aware of all you gave.

Events beyond our control often steal our contentment. The longing that our lives have impact is a godly longing. The desire for pleasant circumstances is natural. But Paul knew where to find the gate to contentment when his life was difficult. In

Philippians he told his friends that he had made a decision. He would look at every circumstance of his life as an opportunity for Jesus to be made known: "I eagerly expect and hope that I will in no way be ashamed, but will have sufficient courage so that now as always Christ will be exalted in my body" (1:20). Living or dying, jailed or free, highly regarded or disdained and forgotten, he had realized it could all be used as a place to showcase Jesus.

A friend wrote in her journal as a young woman, "Lord, let my life be a platform where the beauty of Jesus is revealed." At the time, she thought that prayer would open her world up to some great adventure. Instead her life has always felt small and unimportant. As an only child who has never married, she has struggled both relationally and financially. She's arrived in her forties with no more job security than she had in her twenties. Her elderly parents have less than she does and are counting on her to help them. It seems she will never have a life of her own.

Getting to know her has been a walk alongside a woman who decided she wanted God's presence more than she wanted her problems fixed. It has not been easy. When she was younger, what she did not have dominated her thinking. We spent hours going over how difficult her life was, how much she was counting on the future to bring relief. She poured it out to God and to a couple of close friends.

Time went by; things did not change. But rather than giving up, she began to quiet her heart. She decided that rather than resenting her parents, she would see that part of the calling on her life was to serve them well, despite the ways they had let her down. She quit trying to soothe her heart with frequent trips to the mall. She started a small group for other singles in her apartment. Nothing complicated—she just asked three friends to come to her house every week for coffee and cookies and reading the Bible. She spent a lot of Saturday mornings walking the beach near her home.

Reading one of her old journals, she found the prayer she had written in her twenties: "Let my life be a platform where the beauty of Jesus is revealed." A sense of gratitude began to emerge as she realized her circumstances were her opportunities for exactly that to happen. Regardless of how limited or lonely they may be, they can always be a chance to showcase Jesus. She has learned, in fact, that some of the most beautiful aspects of Christ's character can be revealed only against the backdrop of disappointment. She is content, even thankful, despite her limitations and unmet desires.

Remember King David's story. His deepest longing was for God's people to have a beautiful place in which to worship God. That desire won out over the passion to be the architect, fund-supplier, and master contractor of the project. It was all about God, David realized, not about himself. From that crucible of denied dreams, a transformed man emerged. David meant what he said at the end of his life: God had been very good to him.

THE PROBLEM WITH PEOPLE: AN OPPORTUNITY TO WORSHIP

Circumstances destroy our heart's rest. So do people. In chapter 2 we talked about the disruption that people can bring into our lives. We feel the weight of their expectations; we worry whether they will do right and do well. We struggle to forgive them. But there is more. People are so disappointing. We try (at times, at least) to give them our very best, and nothing much changes. Or the situation gets worse.

Paul knew that firsthand. Like any other place on this planet, the church at Philippi had its fill of pride, selfishness, and conflict. To help these Christians understand how they were to navigate the troubled waters of relationships, Paul highlighted the amazing Jesus, who gave up heaven's glory to take a servant's low place and to die a shameful death.

He also told the story of his own heart in difficult relationships. He knew his calling was to encourage and teach the church, but when he saw them struggling, he wondered, just as we do, if his work was making any difference. Were they changing? Did they understand that he was pouring out his heart for them?

All of us know the feeling. We ride waves of tumult in our relationships. Fears sweep us away as we think of our children. The burden of caring for elderly parents who have turned crotchety and rarely say thank you bears down upon us. We give our best at a church and it splits. We long to mend the growing gulf we see between our children and their father. We give our hearts away in ministry and then wonder if there has been any change anywhere, and if anyone cares about us. It all seems as futile as writing in the sand while the tide rises. How do we live at rest when we are rebuffed, when we only see futility where we had hoped to impart life? How do we live at rest when deep down we long for tenderness and connection in relationships and feel only bored disregard?

To such questions, Paul replied, "But even if I am being poured out like a drink offering . . . I rejoice" (Philippians 2:17). We pour out the best we are, and what's the effect? Seemingly nothing. In Old Testament worship, the burning of whole animal carcasses left a pile of ashes. At other times, the priests reserved part of the sacrificial animals as food for their families. Similarly, the priests ate the offerings of grain after they had been placed on the altar. Every sacrifice but the drink offering had a substance that lingered, something that could be seen, smelt, or tasted after the worship was completed.

But when a drink offering of wine was poured on a burnt offering, it flashed in flame, then disappeared. Paul admitted he was not sure if his ministry was going to produce obvious results in people's lives—perhaps it was as ephemeral as a drink offering. Nonetheless, he chose to rejoice. His rest of heart did not depend on knowing that he had helped people change or on his sense of being blessed and appreciated. His relationships were about something far more cosmic—they were about worship.

Therefore, no matter how difficult or disappointing his relationships were, they could still be a source of gratitude, not frustration. Similarly, by our choice to care, to keep giving our best to another, to be as Jesus would be to her, we worship. That worship brings delight to the heart of God.

Our perspective, however, is often at odds with Paul's perspective. By our involvement in others' lives, by what happens in them, by their love and appreciation of us, we hope to fill up our own hearts. But if these are our hopes, we are looking at our relationships through the wrong lens, expecting other people, by their response to us, to give us the contentment we long for. In reality, though, our hearts grow full only as we realize that our service to others is sheer worship, not a way to earn a payback.

One of the most godly men I know spent the first twenty-five years of his ministry convinced that people would be changed by his love for them and by the truth of God and the power of the Spirit. Yet as the years wore on, he saw young, eager converts decline into middle-aged professionals who had little interest in Jesus Christ. He saw Christian marriages he had deeply respected crumble. He saw churches continue year after year with their bickering and backbiting. Disappointment wearied his soul, wearied his bones. He would not give up Jesus, but he would give up involvement with people.

For a period of time, he really did quit. He showed up or spoke up only when he absolutely had to. As his depression grew into a wall of silence, his wise wife and closest friends gave him time and quiet to sort it through. It was wintertime, and the season itself became a picture of his soul. He would sit for long periods simply thinking about the Scriptures and Jesus. He wasn't planning his next message; he was simply thinking. He played games with his children. He took his wife out for coffee. He made his heart listen week by week as the preacher at his church taught from the book of Hebrews about the incomparable Jesus.

As springtime came, he began to find rest for his heart in the midst of a world he could not fix. Several years have gone by since that time; people haven't changed much. But he lives from a different place. The gate to heart rest in the midst of relationships opened to him. He is grateful, not for what his ministry does for people, but because his involvement in their lives is his opportunity to worship God.

Carol is slowly learning the same lesson. She raised three boys with hardly a hitch, but her fourth child, a girl, has her believing that she'll never get it right being a mother to a daughter. Shauna is fifteen, but the conflict started long before the teen years. Carol finds herself watching the clock all day, dreading the moment when Shauna walks in the door from school. Something always goes wrong; no matter what approach she tries with this child, tears, angry words, shut doors, and sullenness erupt.

Carol's honest talk with an older woman is helping. The choice to tell her story to this woman was humiliating in the beginning. Her boys had been so easy that Carol had always been the one to whom friends came for parenting advice. This older veteran mother understood. Her child-rearing years had been marked by real struggles as well; she knew how hard it often was for women to admit things weren't going well with a child. Her wisdom has helped Carol to move her focus away from the daily ups and downs of her relationship with Shauna. Rather than evaluating everything by Shauna's moods and choices, Carol is determined to be as Jesus would be to this daughter. In the daily sacrifice of learning to be a wise and loving mother, she has an opportunity to be poured out in worship before God.

THE ACHE OF OUR LOSSES: THE PLACE OF INTIMACY

Difficult circumstances and difficult people make it hard to be content, but each can serve as a gate to rich rest of heart. In the same way, the losses we suffer are meant to enlarge our souls. At times, however, we believe there will never be any healing for our losses. Years may go by, but still we rehearse our grief. The soul contentment that leads to rest seems impossible when our losses loom so large.

Paul too experienced the challenge of finding contentment in the midst of his losses. As he opened chapter 3 of Philippians, he cataloged the losses he suffered because of his commitment to know Jesus Christ. Family connection, personal identity, life purpose, recognition, and the community of his peers all crumbled. What he lost was important to him. The Greek word for *gain* really means "cargo." In time he came to see how little value his precious cargo had, but at the time of losing it, the loss stung. Yet he learned to be grateful for his losses because the pain of loss opened his eyes to knowing Jesus Christ in a profound and intimate way. Eugene Peterson's paraphrase captures the powerful hold things and people can have on us and the exuberant freedom Paul found as he let them go:

> The very credentials these people are waving around as something special, I'm tearing up and throwing out with the trash—along with everything else I used to take credit for. And why? Because of Christ. Yes, all the things I once thought were so important are gone from my life. Compared to the high privilege of knowing Christ Jesus as my Master, firsthand, everything I once thought I had going for me is insignificant—dog dung. I've dumped it all in the trash so that I could embrace Christ and be embraced by him. (Philippians 3:7-8, MSG)

Carolyn knows what Paul means. She lost everything in her mid-forties as her husband left, convinced a younger woman would give him the excitement he craved. In the process, her two children turned on her, their hurt turning to anger as they decided she was to blame. While their world slid into drugs and promiscuity, she floundered. For several years she lived so close to the edge of poverty that she had no option but to move in with her elderly and demanding parents, who subtly kept up the blame that she was the one at fault. Finally, she found decent employment so she could provide a home that her children might one day want to return to.

During that time, she sat in church alone, struggling with her losses, struggling against a sense of condemnation. Had God totally abandoned her? After far too many dark months, a friend gently said something that began to clear her vision: "Carolyn, it starts with just one heart." Something rang true in those words. She could live the rest of her life oriented toward her losses, rehearsing them, recalling their pain. Or, she could start with her own heart and get to know the person of Jesus in a way she never had before. She found the same thing Paul found, that when we have all we think we need, our sense of sufficiency obstructs our vision. But when loss invades our world, Jesus has the opportunity to become visible.

In chapter 6 we will take a much longer look at the grief that arises from our losses. When we get there, we will explore how our response to our grief can become a gate to rest of heart. That is another story. What is important at this point is to listen to Paul's testimony. He is not telling us how to handle the grief of our losses; he is affirming for us what our losses can do for us. They are meant to clear our vision, to help us see what is important. As we realize that so much of what we thought matters really doesn't matter at all, we will see how very much a deep connection with Jesus Himself does matter. In the intimacy that arises when we decide we want Him more than we want what we have lost, we find a true home for our hearts. We find rest.

The heart rest we long for flows out of contentment. But our circumstances, the people in our lives, and the losses we experience so often sabotage contentment. Will we waste our lives trying to perfect our circumstances? Will we demand that other people satisfy our hunger for intimacy and meaning? Will we spend our energy endlessly rehearsing our losses? If we do, our heart will never find the rest we crave. The soul fullness that leads to rest matures within us as we learn gratitude. Our difficult circumstances provide an opportunity for Jesus to be showcased through our lives. People give us the opportunity to worship as we are poured out for their benefit. Our losses draw back the veil so that our grieving souls can see Jesus in a way they never have before. As we live by the reality that it takes a lot of thankfulness, the gate swings open to a contented heart of rest.

Taking Time

1. If it truly takes a lot of thankfulness, begin today. For what are you thankful?

2. Greed, envy, and covetousness are not always blatant and ugly. Sit with your own heart in quietness. Where are these deadly things at work in your life?

3. Circumstances, people, losses—in what arena do you struggle with contentment? How can Paul's testimony help you to see your life as opportunity, not disappointment?

5

THE GRIP
OF FEAR

SUMMER MORNINGS IN THE ROCKY MOUNTAINS DAZZLE THE senses, the air glistening with light, the sun sharpening colors so that everything seems newly made. Anna had picked me up before eight; Julie's best time was always early morning. As we drove west out of town, with the mountains looming larger and clearer against the western sky, Anna began to tell me about her friend. Julie's husband was an oncologist. Anna and Julie had met each other through their husbands' work. Julie was just fun, Annie said; even all her teenaged children knew that. Their house hovered at the edge of chaos, four boys in six years and then a little girl. Everything around them overran with possibilities—several horses, two cages of bunnies, two dogs, and several cats. The garage was not accessible by car; with a path down its center, it served as storage for adventures: climbing equipment, kayaks, canoes, cross-country skis, and camping paraphernalia. Something was always on the verge of happening in their lives.

Anna remembered one night when the four adults sat on the wide porch that extended across the back of Julie's house as dusk gathered. The boys had not finished their chores, and the whole group was leaving to go camping the next morning, so two were mowing the grass with headlamps on while the other two boys parked their dad's car so its headlights could illumine the camping trailer they were loading with equipment.

But then three years ago the doctors discovered a sarcoma in Julie's body. It had made its home on her spine. The surgery was dangerous but successful, yet just as things were settling back to normal, Julie's cancer returned. This time it spread to her intestines and then her back. It was just a matter of time, Anna said, but Julie was determined to live every day of it. As we pulled up in front of the house, we found her on the porch, the eastern light streaming across her face, her red sweater mirroring the morning brightness. But it wasn't her beauty; it wasn't the glory of summer mornings in the Rockies; it was something else. Her peace. I had asked Anna earlier that summer if she knew anyone who had faced great fear and found the gate to rest. She had told me about Julie and had asked Julie if she could handle meeting someone new.

Julie had said yes, so now we sat on her porch, ready to talk. We chatted, as women do, and then I asked the question Julie knew I had come to ask: "Julie, you seem so totally at peace. How have you kept fear from consuming you?"

Laughing, she asked if I really did see her that way. At times she had totally lost it, she confessed. Then she began to tell her story. I share it with you now because it is a picture of all of us as we face our deepest fears. Those frightening things, both real and imagined, that would destroy our heart rest have the potential to become the very gate through which we find the peace and love of God.

A DESCENT INTO DARKNESS

Julie began with the facts. She was only forty when doctors found the first cancer. Her children were half grown; she had counted on so many years with them and with her husband, and she felt so very young herself. At the same time, God had made her ready. Earlier that spring, she had experienced the immediate presence of God's love in a way she never had before. Several months after that, driving home alone late one night, she had another profound encounter with God as she realized her health was a gift, not a guarantee, from His good heart.

Medically she was well prepared. Julie was a nurse by training; her husband, an oncologist. He immediately accessed the best care possible. The medical community's personal care for her reflected the respect other doctors had for her husband. Furthermore, she had family support—not just her husband, but parents who could help out and an extended family who genuinely cared.

Finally, with their combined medical background, Julie and her husband could monitor this cancer themselves. Like him, she understood all the numbers, all the jargon; she could compare what her own research told her to the lab work-ups her doctor did, making sure in the process that she was getting the best help available.

Somehow she survived the initial diagnosis, the surgery, and the heavy rounds of chemotherapy. But then the first period of waiting set in. Despite all the reasons she had to hold steady in her heart, fear began to writhe deep in her spirit. Had the cancer really been eradicated? A few months later, blood work came back with elevated levels. She did more research on the Internet, then lost it. In a tidal wave of fear she headed for the emergency room, insisting they draw blood, do another work-up, and begin a more aggressive treatment. But when the doctors on duty saw her state of mind, they called her husband to come get her and take her home.

The drive home was terrible, Julie said. She felt like her husband had betrayed her, her body had betrayed her, and God Himself had turned on her. All that was left was the fear. And the cancer. When she arrived home, she went straight to her room.

She would not come out for supper; she would not let her husband talk to her. For almost a week she lived in total isolation, fighting the terror. She was going to die. Not for sure, but probably.

In that week as she refused all human comfort, reality forced its way into her soul. She could not build a fortress strong enough to guarantee her protection. But in that room, another awareness began to grow. God was there. He had not walked away in disgust because she had handled her fear so poorly. Somehow, no matter what happened in two months or two years or ten, He would still be there. She also began to think a lot about heaven. With a life as full as hers, heaven had been the fall-back plan, a vague and future reality. But the more she thought, the more she began to realize that heaven was a present reality. A good chance existed that her body was going to betray her. But even if it did, God wouldn't; He would be right beside her through it all, ready to welcome her into that real place called heaven.

When she first came out of the bedroom, her family gathered around, filled with their own fears that she wouldn't be able to handle the future. But in the months that followed, as she realized how near God was, how real heaven was, God Himself began weaving peace into her soul. Not a peace tied to guarantees that life would turn out a certain way, but a peace anchored in the very heart of God.

Now, two years later, I sat with this same woman on her porch, enjoying a cup of tea and the summer morning as she explained what she was learning through her continuing fight with cancer. Anna was right—in the midst of terrible uncertainties, her friend Julie had let her fears open the gate to rest of heart.

SOUL TURBULENCE: THE HINDRANCE AT THE DOOR TO REST

Before we look at what Julie learned, we need to think about our own hearts. Our stories may be very different from hers, but many of us know the soul turbulence that fear produces. When we are afraid, our fear insists that we cannot rest until we receive a guarantee that the terrible thing we dread will not happen. As we attempt to handle our anxious hearts, we are convinced that nobody could live in rest if they were facing the things we are facing.

On the other hand, your experience may not feel like turbulence at all. Perhaps for you life has a backdrop of a steady inner gnawing. You would never classify yourself as frantic or obsessive, but low-grade anxiety has attached itself to your very being. If you are going to learn to lead your heart to rest, you too must come face to face with worry's power to shape your soul.

Whether your heart is reeling with fear or suffering from the constant drag of anxious thoughts, you understand Julie as she faced her cancer. How can a person experience the shift of heart that Julie experienced? Is it possible to live from peace when the issues that have caused such deep disquiet remain unresolved? The truth of Scripture is that God intends for the very fear we cannot solve to open the gate to a life of rest. As Julie told me how her soul had made that shift from anxiety to peace, I realized I had heard her story before. The choices she faced in that time of fear are the same choices the nation of Israel faced at a frightening time in its history. As we examine what God said to His people when they were overcome with terror, we will see how He spoke to Julie in the midst of her cancer and how He longs to speak to us as well.

OBSTINATE OR TRUSTING?

After David and Solomon were dead, Judah (the southern kingdom of divided Israel) had growing opportunities for worry. Weakened in their relationship with God because of sin, the Judeans (or Jews) experienced threatening pressure from more-powerful nations around them. By the time of the prophet Isaiah, this pressure had escalated into a bondage of fear.

The Jews did what came naturally. They sought a solution, a way to protect themselves from frightening possibilities. Egypt looked like a logical place to find a dependable ally. An ancient and powerful country, Egypt boasted a well-developed culture, military might, and a highly organized government. Furthermore, an alliance with Judah would help Egypt. The Egyptians also recognized the threat the Assyrians posed and reasoned that a strong Judah to their north would provide them with a buffer.

The true prophets of God, however, were dead-set against such alliances. They called the Jews again and again to put their trust in God, not in other nations. God had His own impeccable proof that He was completely trustworthy. Years earlier, when Egypt was at the height of her power, God had trampled her army as He freed His people from slavery to the Pharaoh. He then led His people into the Promised Land under Joshua's leadership, giving them an almost unbroken string of victories. Later, through David, God again gave His people abundant victory.

By Isaiah's time, though, the immediate pressure from fierce enemies obscured all God had done. In view of Judah's distress, how could anyone refute the logic of making an alliance with a powerful nation? God is invisible; He often waits until the last minute to help. Egypt was visible, obviously mighty. She made promises one could actually hear.

"Woe to the obstinate children,"
     declares the LORD,
"to those who carry out plans that are not mine,
     forming an alliance, but not by my Spirit,
     heaping sin upon sin;
who go down to Egypt
     without consulting me;
who look for help to Pharaoh's protection,
     to Egypt's shade for refuge.

But Pharaoh's protection will be to your shame,
 Egypt's shade will bring you disgrace. . . .
Because you have rejected this message,
 relied on oppression
 and depended on deceit,
this sin will become for you
 like a high wall, cracked and bulging,
 that collapses suddenly, in an instant.
It will break in pieces like pottery,
 shattered so mercilessly
that among its pieces not a fragment will be found
 for taking coals from a hearth
 or scooping water out of a cistern." (Isaiah 30:1-5,12-14)

Judah's inclination, like ours, was to trust what could be seen and heard. Isaiah thundered against this choice. In Isaiah 36, the intensity of the prophet's desire for the people to understand how reliable, how true, how good God was, even in the midst of their greatest fears, reached an intense climax.

We are no different from Judah. We gravitate toward tangible assurances and human solutions to control the frightening things we face. However, this default system takes us further from trust in God. We are obstinate children, Isaiah says, when we exhaust every resource rather than turning to God for help.

Think about Julie. She was determined to control her fears by knowledge. It's true for all of us. Whether we make an alliance with knowledge, with control, or with doing life perfectly, whether we manipulate, or whether we blast our fears with our anger, the issue is the same. We are seeking for something that will look and feel more substantial than trust in the invisible God.

Furthermore, just like the Jews, we do not see that our protection schemes take us further away from God; from our perspective they look so rational. It made sense to Julie to turn to her Internet research, to scrutinize her lab results again and again.

But God says through Isaiah that we are wrong. It is stubbornness in our hearts when we refuse to remember how good and powerful He is and when we do not take into account that He has promised to be present in our most overwhelming situations. If we don't listen, as Isaiah so graphically warned, the very things we attempt to trust will shatter; our lives will become like broken walls and shards of pottery. We have all watched the things we thought we could trust disintegrate before our very eyes. Sooner or later the reality comes home to each of us: there is no defense we can build in this life that sorrow and trouble cannot penetrate.

So what do we do? Live in fear and defeat? Do we embrace cynicism, telling ourselves that bad things always happen, so what's the use? Isaiah's proposal was radically different. Listen to His solution to our fears, the solution Julie came to comprehend: "In repentance and rest is your salvation, in quietness and trust is your strength" (Isaiah 30:15).

What does it mean to adopt these four attitudes of heart: repentance, rest, quietness, and trust?

REPENTANCE

Repentance means "returning; going back to the beginning point." As we work our way through our fears, we must decide what will be the underlying assumption or starting place for our understanding of life. Julie said during our conversation that her deepest questions circled around God's character. Could He be trusted, or had He betrayed her? The battle over whether she would be mastered by her fears or learn to live out of a heart of rest began with what she believed about God's heart. This is the starting point for us as well.

God is good. He has demonstrated that throughout the pages of Scripture, and ultimately at the cross. Do we believe Him, or do we insist on minute-by-minute, experiential verification of that truth? If God's goodness is constantly up for evaluation, then the only way to measure that goodness is by the constant experience of a pleasurable, relatively problem-free, and do-able life.

REST

Rest pushes us even further. In the Hebrew it means "descent; receiving with humility." When we fight fearful things, when we seek to control them with human weapons, we are, as Isaiah says, obstinate children who insist that life work out our way. Job understood that. After he lost everything, his wife urged him to curse God and die. His response arose from a heart that was at rest in the midst of great grief: "You are talking like a foolish woman. Shall we accept good from God, and not trouble?" (Job 2:10).

Choosing to live out of rest in the midst of our fears means we take the child's position, the position of the receiver. We trust God's heart even when He won't guarantee outcomes.

QUIETNESS

Quietness takes us still deeper into rest. To be quiet means to come to an end; to be totally spent. Quietness does not mean we never panic, but it does mean we are learning to entrust our fears to the Father's heart. Psalm 131 provides a graphic picture of quietness:

My heart is not proud, O LORD,
    my eyes are not haughty;
I do not concern myself with great matters
    or things too wonderful for me.
But I have stilled and quieted my soul;
    like a weaned child with its mother,
    like a weaned child is my soul within me.

O Israel, put your hope in the LORD
    both now and forevermore.

Anyone familiar with the ways of a nursing baby understands David's analogy. An infant that has grown accustomed to his mother's breast often fights the weaning process. Can't you imagine the internal feelings a small one might have: "Here I am, frustrated-angry-panicked-mad. I'm on my mother's lap, her arms are around me, but she won't give me what I love, what I've grown accustomed to, what I need." I remember my own children fighting the weaning process, becoming almost frantic in their insistence that they must nurse.

Yet in her wisdom and love, the mother knows the time to stand firm against her child's demands. As she resists his desire, a moment comes when the child quiets himself. Somehow, mysteriously, without words being shared, that child makes the decision to trust the heart of the mother and to trust the arms that hold him, even though that same person is refusing to give him what he most wants.

Amazingly, the Hebrew word for *wean* has a secondary meaning; it can also mean "to deal bountifully with." Weaning is a denial, but it is also a process of dealing bountifully with a child. No one can stay forever at the breast and grow to maturity. Weaning pushes us toward growth. Our fears insist, *You cannot handle life if this thing happens. What will you do if this other thing you long for never comes into being?* In quietness we remind ourselves that we choose to trust the One who holds us, even though we do not understand His ways. As our souls are quieted, our bounteous God opens a gate to fullness of heart in the midst of our fears.

CONFIDENCE

Confidence is the final heart place to which Isaiah calls the frightened Israelites. This confidence does not arise from our own sense of security. The word means "a place of refuge." Isaiah does not ask us to muster up an indomitable spirit, but challenges us to decide whom or what we will really trust. The people of Judah were looking to Egypt for safety despite Isaiah's warning that this shield would crumble. Similarly, most of the things we turn to cannot protect us.

We confront this reality again and again as we face our fears. Homeschooling and Christian schools can't guarantee Christlike children. Stock options and well-balanced portfolios aren't a high wall against economic downturns. Great grades in graduate school may not mean a great job once we're finished. Exercise and healthy eating don't necessarily produce long and healthy lives. Living in America cannot protect you from terrorists. Trying hard and praying may not save your marriage. Even the best things are only broken walls and pottery shards if we rely on them for protection. When our human solutions are inadequate, when the future is up for grabs, the only thing that quiets fear is knowing that God is a true refuge. He is available in every difficulty.

Repentance, rest, quietness, confidence. If we embrace these choices in the midst of our fears, then troubles can become the gate to God's heart. His rest will be for us a secure home in an insecure world. As our fears make us needy, we have the opportunity to see how utterly available God is to us.

But as Isaiah so bluntly pointed out, the people of Judah would have none of it. They were determined to solve their fears on their own. In His mercy, God had more than just rebuke for them. God, said Isaiah, "longs to be gracious to you; he rises to show you compassion" (Isaiah 30:18). The Hebrew language blazes with imagery. The phrase literally reads: *God stands on tiptoe to show you tender mercy.* When we see only the things that terrify us, we have missed the truest thing of all: God on tiptoe, watching, waiting for the slightest cue from us, ready to enter in.

> O people of Zion . . . How gracious he will be when you cry for help! As soon as he hears, he will answer you. . . . Whether you turn to the right or to the left, your ears will hear a voice behind you, saying, "This is the way; walk in it." (Isaiah 30:19,21)

God longed to use the very things the Jews feared to forge a life of blessing and healing. It is true for us as well. In the process, several decisions face us.

WHAT DO WE EXPECT LIFE TO BE?

First of all, we have to ask ourselves, *What do we really expect life to be?* A place where all prayers are answered immediately? A place where we know well in advance that we will have all the resources we need to meet every challenge? A place where none of the scary possibilities that wound and destroy other people will ever happen to us? We long for that first garden in Eden, but a life of endless ease is a cheap substitute. So what is the good life?

Paul said, "The righteous will live by faith" (Galatians 3:11). The implications of his statement go far beyond our salvation. The most alive life is the one lived by faith. From the definition of faith in Hebrews 11:1, we learn that faith is the firm conviction that what we see around us isn't all there is to reality and that what we presently possess isn't all that will one day be ours. If we believe this, the implications are cosmically frightening and wonder-filled at the same time. To live by faith means that invisible spiritual realities and promises about the future will give my heart strength. It means I acknowledge that blessings and assurances in the present material world are not the gate to true heart rest.

We need a faith like that. Life is shot through with fearful things. Your child is out with friends on a snowy January evening and the falling snow develops into an icy rain. He's past his curfew, and you find your heart tightening. Does faith mean a guarantee that there will be no car accident? Or does it mean you know your child is in God's hands no matter what happens out on the road? Does faith mean you won't be laid off, or does it mean you will have the inner resources to survive joblessness? Does it mean your husband won't have an affair, or that God will hold you in His arms even if the worst happens?

Our fears rarely have present-tense answers—that's why the choice to live by faith is the only way out of the stronghold of worry. Angie's life is an extreme example, but her decision to live by faith is the same one we must make. Three years ago she married; two years ago she was diagnosed with acute leukemia. Research across North America produced a donor for bone marrow. Surviving the near-death agony of that procedure, Angie began to envision life stretching out before her once more.

Less than a year later her blood marrow cells began to falter. Two subsequent tests gave disturbing news. But it was Christmas; despite her fatigue, she was determined to buy something beautiful for her husband. He needed a new suit, so she searched the mall until she found a lovely black one, on sale, perfect for the man she loved. As she watched the salesman ring up the charge and slip a plastic cover over the gift, tears sprung into her eyes. Without warning, the thought flashed through her head, *He'll probably wear it to my funeral.*

We were chatting about how she was doing in late January. "Do you know what I've learned?" she said, "I've learned the only real living is by faith. Everybody that is really living is living the same way—a life-by-faith. Their struggles, their issues, may be different from mine, but God isn't asking me to do any more than anyone else." That truth has formed a place for her to be at rest, a place to be with God in the midst of the very real fears that the leukemia is still seeking her life.

If we want more than an existence where we attempt to hem in and protect ourselves and those we love, the only recourse we have is faith—the choice to trust the goodness of God in the face of a very imperfect and incomplete reality.

WILL WE PERSIST?

The second issue we must face if our fears are to become the gateway to rest is to realize that faith is not passivity. Our fears roam about inside our hearts or explode into our consciousness as we awaken, so we lie wide-eyed and anxious in the dark. Our fears keep us from our work and skew our relationships. Obviously, a faith that just says "let go" will never dispel the tyranny of worry. At one time the pressure on King David's life became so severe that he responded as we often do:

> Oh that I had the wings of a dove!
> I would fly away and be at rest—
> I would flee far away
> and stay in the desert. . . . I would hurry to
> my place of shelter,
> far from the tempest and storm. (Psalm 55:6-8)

In the midst of our worry, all we want is out; all we want is for God to solve it. Despite his longings, David faced his fears, taking them back to God again and again. Eventually, the battle inside him began to subside. His testimony is not that of a man who once and for all released his fears into God's hands, but rather that of a man who turned back to God each time the tide of fear rose in his soul.

> Evening, morning and noon
> I cry out in distress,
> and he hears my voice.
> He ransoms me unharmed
> from the battle waged against me,
> even though many oppose me. (Psalm 55:17-18)

The gate to the rest we long for in the midst of our fears is gained only by persistence. Again and again, as our hearts fill up with fear, we return to the God who is ever patient, who never shames us for our faltering, whose heart is always open wide.

DO WE WANT THE GIFT OF PEACE?

Finally, if repentance, rest, quietness, and confidence are to shape our hearts, we must make an honest self-appraisal. Do we really want the gift of peace in the midst of our fears? Or do we insist that God solve our problems so that our rest flows from what He has done for us?

Sometimes our worry is the thread by which we hang onto the belief that we can do something to change our situation and end our fear. As ridiculous as it is, we believe that our anxiety gives us some measure of control. Or we believe it keeps God mindful of our problem. We are afraid that without the pressure of our fear, He might forget what we want from Him. But our anxiety and demanding prayers accomplish nothing. We fear giving up our fear because if we don't worry, who will remember to care? If we don't worry, would God decide we really aren't concerned about the issue? If we don't worry, are we giving up hope of God involving Himself in our world?

Cutting across all our stubborn reasons for remaining in our fear, Paul wrote, "May the God of hope fill you with all joy and peace as you trust in him, so that you may overflow with hope by the power of the Holy Spirit" (Romans 15:13). God's joy and peace are available to us as we trust Him; they are not the result of absolute guarantees about the outcomes of our worries. We have a choice: will we trust Him and receive His joy and peace, or will we insist on seeking our joy and peace from resolved fears and changed circumstances?

A father who understood the significance of letting go of fear in order to receive the gift of joy wrote a letter to his daughter. With their permission I give you a portion of his wise words:

> Underneath the idea of *carpe diem* is the concept that you do not need to fear the will of God. I know there is a strong tendency in all of us to hold out for control

because we are fundamentally afraid that God is going to rip us off if we really let Him be God of our whole lives. He'll take away what we really want and make our lives dull and prosaic. There is no reason to resist Him today. There is nothing gained in delaying the best that God offers us. Bottom line, God is really good, and you have no need to fear Him.

So the choice really is ours. We can hang onto our fears, insisting that until they are resolved, there is no way for us to enter into rest, or we can see those same fears as the door by which we can enter a rest far richer and sweeter than the rest that might arise from a tenuous arrangement of perfect circumstances. That rest flows out of the security of our relationship with God. It is a rest that believes that a life without all the pieces in place, a life in which we do indeed suffer lack, is still a life to celebrate, a good gift from a good God. Yes, the choice is difficult, but if we lay down our fears, choosing instead the heart and the arms of God, the gate will open to rest.

Taking Time

1. Ponder the four words Isaiah gives to a fearful nation: repentance, rest, quietness, confidence. Which word most clearly speaks to the anxiety of your own heart?

2. Honestly speaking, what do you expect life to be? In what area of your life is God calling you to live by faith rather than sight?

3. If persistent fears block your way to rest, what does it mean to deal persistently with those fears?

4. What do you long for most: the gift of peace, or a promise that your fears won't come true? Take your answer to this question back to the Father.

LISTENING TO MY TEARS

I DID NOT CRY FOR MY FATHER UNTIL SEPTEMBER. HE TOOK HIS life on a scorching day in early June, his body worn out from unrelenting pain and his mind frayed by far too many drugs given by doctors to heal his agony. The sheer immensity of the sorrow, the terror of a universe that now held no guarantees, log-jammed my soul. Tears were impossible. I loved him so much. I was his only daughter, and he had been the plumb line for tenderness and goodness all my growing-up life. He loved me; I had known that since I knew anything. He was supposed to be my hero and fight the impossible pain until somehow he brought pain to its knees. He was my husband's friend, my children's grandfather, my mother's true husband.

Suicide had already marked my larger family. Part of my father's job had been to keep it from touching us. He was young, only fifty-eight. He was a Christian, but now he had obliterated all my categories for understanding God by succumbing to pain's temptation.

I could never again call him, never again take my children by his office to discover the little gifts he had stashed in his bottom desk drawer. He would never again sit at the table in the corner, the one in front of all the windows, and read his Bible.

In place of all that had been was the oppressive emptiness of a universe with no answers. Inside me was grief so large that it could find no way out. It pressed against my heart, pressed against my guts, until I thought my whole life would be spent just carrying it.

One fall morning, the dammed-up sorrow broke. I had taken my children to school. Alone in the car on my way home, I was listening to music, strategizing how to make it through one more day. What triggered the rupture of my heart that morning; what made it possible to cry? I still don't know. But I pulled off the road and wept until I thought my own soul had been washed from my body in all the tears. But I was wrong. That morning was only the beginning. The heaviness morphed into months of tears. But between the tears was no relief, only piles and piles of questions that still had no answers.

Like a sailboat becalmed in an ocean of grief, I saw the same vista in every direction: a sea of hurting spread out in an unending circle around me. The testimony of other people caught up in their sorrows spoke to my heart in ways that no one else was able to. C. S. Lewis could not find answers to his questions in the months following his wife's death:

> Meanwhile, where is God? This is one of the most disquieting symptoms. When you are happy, so happy that you have no sense of needing Him, so happy that you are tempted to feel His claim upon you as an interruption, if you remember yourself, and turn to Him with gratitude and praise, you will be—or so it feels—welcomed with open arms. But go to Him when your need is desperate, when all other help is vain, and what to you find? A door slammed in your face, a sound of bolting and double on the inside. After that, silence.[1]

At some point during those months I found Psalm 88, and the rawness of the emotions it expressed shocked me. Unlike earthly leaders, God apparently had no need to edit what was said about Him. Psalm 88 writhed with the overwhelming blackness of a pain that begged for God's help. I read it again and again, amazed that God offered nothing in response, no correction, no comfort, no relief. The psalm felt like the cycle of my days, concluding in the same agony with which they began.

For my soul is full of trouble
　　and my life draws near the grave. . . .
You have put me in the lowest pit,
　　in the darkest depths.
Your wrath lies heavily upon me;
　　you have overwhelmed me with all your waves. . . .
I am confined and cannot escape;
　　my eyes are dim with grief. . . .
But I cry to you for help, O LORD;
　　in the morning my prayer comes before you.
Why, O LORD, do you reject me
　　and hide your face from me? . . .
I have suffered your terrors and am in despair.
　　. . . your terrors have destroyed me.
　　. . . the darkness is my closest friend.
　　　　　　　　　　(Psalm 88:3,6-9,13-16,18)

So where is God when it hurts that badly? Does He stand at the side, politely impatient when our tears are flowing, waiting until our sorrow is over? Is it possible to have a heart at rest and a broken heart at the same time? Can grief itself open the gate to rest?

That autumn I began to learn for myself that grief is meant to become a gate through which I could find a garden rich with rest.

PRESENT TO OURSELVES

We begin the walk to rest in the midst of our grief as we deter-mine to simply be present to our sorrow, no matter how much it costs. The power of our emotions needs to just stand. If we spir-itualize or minimize what we feel, God cannot use our grief to do a true work of rest in us. We cannot avoid our grief and move directly into rest by spiritual willpower. We have to begin where we are, in the middle of it. God in His mercy let me see this real-ity shortly before my father's death.

In early spring of that same year, I read an article on grief by Ingrid Trobisch, a South African woman. She began by describ-ing her experience of losing a close friend. Although she did her best in an intensely spiritual manner to handle the loss, her heart felt no relief. Her grief turned into a darkness that grew rather than diminished, and all her spiritual striving could not alleviate her sorrow. During this struggle, her husband offered her this simple advice: "Ingrid, let the deep hurt hurt." Hearing the truth of God in what he said, she decided to let the grief do its work in her. As she learned to grieve her grief, rather than fight it with a superficial spirituality, the gateway back into life opened for her again. Not long after, the most unexpected loss descended upon her. Her beloved husband died suddenly. The enormity of the loss and the shock of his dying well before old age hit like a tidal wave. But she followed her husband's wisdom from her previous struggle: *Let the deep hurt hurt.*

Some of us rarely let our hurt hurt. Instead we manage to lock it up in remote corners of our souls. This strategy is appeal-ing, even spiritual in appearance. For example, the sadness from two abortions in her twenties hovered in the back corners of Margaret's soul, but she usually managed to keep these memo-ries and emotions confined to a tight, private corner of her heart. She was busy, a relentless perfectionist, a diligent wife and mother. One of the abortions occurred after her marriage; yet her husband refused to discuss it. She knew if she went down that road, his anger and her tears would combine to produce a Grand Canyon-sized chasm between them.

Afraid of what might happen and determined to get over it, she turned as fully as she could to her faith. Technically, she knew she was forgiven, but she couldn't get past the sadness and the guilt. Mostly, she felt trapped. To go near the pain sounded like an opportunity for pain to multiply, but to keep it locked up was killing her.

Margaret was an accomplished musician, and it occurred to her one day that refusing to face the grief and shame was like refusing to play the low notes on a piano. Then, in order to keep balance, her soul also had lost its ability to play the high notes, to reach those delightful places of joy. Her life had become a lifeless melody, played only on the three notes clustered around middle C. The music of her existence was boring, predictable, proper — just like her heart. She was afraid: would God really be there to pick up the pieces if she let the deep hurt out and let it hurt?

Making the decision she would trust Him for just that, she pulled back from the jumble of activities and relationships that kept her mind distracted and disconnected from her heart. For long periods each day, she sat with her Bible in her lap, reading and praying, letting her heart find a home in the heart of God. She went for long bike rides with her younger daughter in the baby seat behind her, teaching her the nursery-rhyme songs her own mother had taught her.

When she broke her code of silence and shared her story with a couple of close friends, she found, to her great surprise, compassion and acceptance. Over time she developed the courage to look at the darkness of what she'd done. She mourned for those two lost children. Again and again she let the deep hurt hurt until it lost its power.

In a conversation we were having recently, I asked her to try to describe the process. Margaret said it was like finding herself in a dark and scary tunnel. In front of her she could see light shining through, around the edges of a door. But when she reached for the door handle to get out of the tunnel, she found the door locked. Fighting the locked door changed nothing. As she gave up that struggle, she understood what she had to do. The key to the locked door was in the tunnel with her, but back at the other end, in the darkest place. To unlock the door, she would have to make her way back through the darkness, find the key, then bring it back to the locked door. Only then would she be able to find her way to the light.

Gerald Sittser, a professor of religion at Whitworth College, describes his own journey through devastating loss in his book *A Grace Disguised*. His advice affirms Margaret's experience and the counsel Walter Trobisch gave to his wife, Ingrid. In one crushing moment as Sittser's family was traveling on a deserted road, a vehicle driven by a drunk driver hit their van, killing his wife, his four-year-old daughter, and his mother. Sittser was left to raise his three remaining children alone. Listen to his counsel:

> Later my sister Diane told me that the quickest way for anyone to reach the sun and the light of day is not to run west, chasing after the setting sun, but to head east, plunging into the darkness until one comes to the sunrise.
>
> I discovered in that moment that I had the power to choose the direction my life would head, even if the only choice open to me, at least initially, was either to run from the loss or to face it as best I could. Since I knew that darkness was inevitable and unavoidable, I decided from that point on to walk into the darkness rather than try to outrun it, to let my experience of loss take me on a journey wherever it would lead, to allow myself to be transformed by my suffering rather than to think I could somehow avoid it. I chose to turn toward

the pain, however falteringly, and to yield to the loss, though I had no idea at the time what that would mean.[2]

PRESENT TO GOD

Let your tears flow like a river
    day and night;
give yourself no relief,
    your eyes no rest.
Arise, cry out in the night,
    as the watches of the night begin;
pour out your heart like water
    in the presence of the Lord. (Lamentations 2:18-19)

Letting the deep hurt hurt can be terribly destructive if it is done away from the presence of God. It is possible to get stuck in our grief. Recently, I asked an acquaintance who had been widowed two years earlier how she was doing. She reached for my hand, and her eyes filled with tears. "Sally," she said, "it gets harder every day." It is not enough just to grieve. Scripture urges us not just to pour out our hearts, but to pour them out in the presence of the Lord. God longs to be at home with us in our grief.

Yet I have struggled in my own life with how much God really wants to listen. This last year has brought a wave of sorrow to my family. Some mornings I wake up and the hurt seems bigger than it did the day before. Sometimes I wonder if God is weary of listening to me. But when I look at King David, a man who delighted the heart of God, I see a man free to be honest before his God. Three times in his life, despite overwhelming grief, David still knew that God would listen.

A BURNED CITY
David experienced great loss at a place called Ziklag. He and his men had garrisoned their families there, but enemies took

advantage of David's absence. They pillaged and burned the town, taking all the women and children captive. When he saw the burned, empty village,

> David and his men wept aloud until they had no strength left to weep. . . . [He] was greatly distressed because the men were talking of stoning him; each one was bitter in spirit because of his sons and daughters. (1 Samuel 30:4,6)

David's loss, his sense of responsibility for the losses his men were experiencing, and his now precarious position as their leader heaped together into a great outpouring of grief. As David let the torrent inside his soul pour out, he turned a corner: "David was greatly distressed. . . . But [he] found strength in the LORD his God" (1 Samuel 30:4,6).

A LOST BABY

Years later, David's illegitimate child by Bathsheba became very ill. David was so distraught that the palace servants worried about his mental stability. When the child died, his servants hesitated to bring him the news, fearing that the finality of death might send him over the edge. But David sensed in their worried whispers that his son had died. He was lying on the ground pouring his heart out to God, but when he learned the child had died, he got up, washed, and put on fresh clothes so that he could go before God in worship. Then he asked for food. His servants were astonished by their king's renewed strength. But his vision had cleared.

> While the child was still alive, I fasted and wept. I thought, "Who knows? The LORD may be gracious to me and let the child live." But now that he is dead, why should I fast? Can I bring him back again? I will go to him, but he will not return to me. (2 Samuel 12:22-23)

David's heart is a heart cleansed of grief after expressing that grief to God.

A DEAD SON

Still later, David's rebellious son Absalom was killed in a civil war against him. From the perspective of David's generals, Absalom's death was a victory. But because David loved him with an unreasonable passion, he could not bring himself to see the situation for what it was. His grief threatened to destroy him, stealing his desire to live so that he forgot his calling to care for his people. Joab, David's friend, confidante, and top general, intervened with blistering words:

> Today you have humiliated all your men, who have just saved your life. . . . You love those who hate you and hate those who love you. You have made it clear today that the commanders and their men mean nothing to you. I see that you would be pleased if Absalom were alive today and all of us were dead. Now go out and encourage your men. I swear by the LORD that if you don't go out, not a man will be left with you by nightfall. This will be worse for you than all the calamities that have come upon you from your youth till now. (2 Samuel 19:5-7)

Even when David's grief became unreasonable, God sent help. His honesty before God did not mean that God would let his world spin out of control.

Apart from the presence of God, there is no deep healing for our grief. Time can make it easier, but that is all. The good news when our hearts are broken is that God invites us to freely mourn in the great space of His loving presence. Our pain does not threaten Him; it does not cause Him to fear that we will ruin His reputation. He is not repulsed with the ugliness we feel.

Even when we hurt so much that we can hardly bear it, we are still His beloved.

THE GOD WHO DOES NOT WALK AWAY

If we let the deep hurt hurt, will it go on forever? And what about God—maybe we can take our hurt to Him initially, but will He eventually lose patience with us and walk away? The good news is that as we choose to let our grief pierce us, we have the opportunity to find that God walks beside us in the midst of it. We often find that hard to believe, because many times other people cannot handle our sorrow. Their withdrawal can be one of the hardest things to bear.

We had moved to a new city six weeks before my father died. In the four years that followed, I struggled; for the first time in my life, I was unable to make a true friend among the women my age. At the end of those four years, we were moving again. An older woman who had befriended me took me out for lunch right before we left. We had never discussed the fact that I had no close friends, but she brought it up that day. "Do you know why you couldn't make a friend here, Sally?" she asked gently as we sat after lunch, enjoying a cup of coffee. I told her I had no idea. I really didn't. She continued, "The pain on your face was so great that the women your own age were afraid of you."

I knew she must be right. What she said was not cruel; it was not a judgment statement against me or against any of the young women I had met in those four years. It was just the way people are. But God is different. David knew that: "The LORD is close to the brokenhearted," he wrote, "and saves those who are crushed in spirit"(Psalm 34:18). As we let the deep hurt hurt, as we realize that the God who walks in the midst of our pain will never leave us, we can begin to discover how we can recover our souls.

Recovering Our Souls As Our Tears Still Flow

We have the same luxury as David to pour out our hearts before God. We too can deeply grieve our losses, spending ourselves in a flood of regret for what has happened or what will never be. At the same time, God gives us guardrails to keep our grief from destroying us. At times those restraints come from friends. That's what Joab did for David when he saw that David's grief was not leading to rest of heart, but only to a destructive downward spiral.

But sometimes we may not have an honest friend like Joab. When we are alone and over our heads in grief, Asaph, the writer of Psalm 73, can give us counsel. What is his advice?

Take It to the Right Place

Asaph says that ultimately, our angry grief, our unending questions, our deep sadness can be answered only by God Himself. No one can bear the whole weight of our sorrows, and our fiercest grief can even hurt the people we love. Only God has rest of heart to give. Therefore, Aspah made a pledge:

> If I had said, "I will speak thus,"
>   I would have betrayed your children.
> When I tried to understand this,
>   it was oppressive to me
> till I entered the sanctuary of God;
>   then I understood their final destiny. (Psalm 73:15-17)

We do well to listen to Asaph's resolve. We live in a world that is far too weighted toward a free expression of whatever we feel. We excuse ourselves when our words have gone too far, not with a true apology, but with the defensive comeback, "Well, that's just how I feel." But this reply does not absolve us from responsibility for the impact our words may have. Asaph's decision to take his heart to God rather than to other people did not mean he cut himself off from being honest, but it did mean he recognized limits. God can always handle our hearts. Other people sometimes cannot. The burden inside of us may be too large for them to bear.

And even if they can bear it in some sense, our grief is always particularly our own. Sittser explains the loneliness of all grief:

> Loss is a universal experience. Like physical pain, we know it is real because sooner or later all of us experience it. But loss is also a solitary experience. Again, like physical pain, we know it is real only because we experience it uniquely within ourselves. When a person says, "You just don't know what I have gone through and how much I have suffered," we must acknowledge that he or she is entirely correct. We do not know and cannot know. But then again, that person will never know what we have gone through and how much we have suffered either. . . . That is why suffering loss is a solitary experience. That is also why each of us must ultimately face it alone. No one can deliver us, substitute for us, or mitigate the pain for us.[3]

LET OUR PERSPECTIVE BE TRANSFORMED

As we realize we cannot spew out on the people around us the full measure of our grief, and as we realize that even the ones closest to us cannot carry our grief for us, we find we are forced into a narrow channel. The choice before us is more than whether we will turn toward or away from the Father. We face a more fundamental decision than that: whose perspective will we adopt in our grief? Asaph made his choice:

When I tried to understand this,
> it was oppressive to me
till I entered the sanctuary of God;
> then I understood their final destiny. (Psalm 73:15-17)

There is ultimately only one place where our vision is true: in the presence of God. David's highest-ranking soldiers could not comfort him at Ziklag. His palace servants had no answers when he faced a dying child. Joab could rebuke him over his excessive grief for Absalom, but he could not heal him.

If God is to become our home, our place of rest in the midst of grief no human can cure, then the channel must be narrowed. We must come to the point when we realize that God is our only full comforter, our only true healer. Through Him alone will our grief open into a new place of rest.

The great disconnect for most of us is that we know the theological formula. We know we are to take the burdens of our heart to God; we know He has comfort and wisdom and understanding past that of any person. The trouble is that we don't take our real selves to God. We take the religious persona with which we operate. But we have to empty out all the pockets of our lives before God, baring our hearts in His presence if His comfort is going to touch and permeate our souls.

As our grief opens the gate to a whole new world of rest, we will learn as Asaph learned that God is our true home.

Whom have I in heaven but you?
> And earth has nothing I desire besides you.
My flesh and my heart may fail,
> but God is the strength of my heart
> and my portion forever. (Psalm 73:25-26)

I had a childhood friend who lived in the countryside outside the town where I grew up. A small spring bubbled to the earth's surface on the back side of their property. When we were ten years old, her father decided to build a pond by digging out the ground around the spring. He explained that as the spring kept flowing, it would fill the hole that he was cutting into the ground.

For several weekends in a row, I sat with my friend under the shade of a massive oak tree and watched her father use his farm machinery to dig that hole. I found myself not believing what he had told us. The meadow around the spring was not being transformed into a pond. From my perspective, it was only becoming a scarred place of mud and torn-up grass. We had played in that meadow, ridden horses across it, but he was making it ugly.

Over the next few months, the hole began to fill with the water from the spring. By the next year, the pond was full. A new landscape had emerged: the quiet pond, the healed grass of the meadow around it, the huge oak tree, and the red barn in the distance. The gouging of the land had turned a tiny stream into a pond of peace. By God's design, that is the work that grief is meant to do in our lives. Listen to Sittser again as he describes that full place that opened up for him as he let his deep hurt hurt and took his grief into the presence of God:

> Yet the grief I feel is sweet as well as bitter. I still have a sorrowful soul; yet I wake up every morning joyful, eager for what the new day will bring. Never have I felt as much pain as I have in the last three years; yet never have I experienced as much pleasure in simply being alive and living an ordinary life. Never have I felt so broken; yet never have I felt so whole. Never have I been so aware of my weakness and vulnerability; yet never have I been so content and so strong. Never has my soul been more dead; yet never has my soul been more alive. What I once considered mutually exclusive—sorrow and joy, pain and pleasure, death and life—have become parts of a greater whole. My soul has been stretched.[4]

Taking Time

1. Have you ever let the deep hurt hurt? Where did it take you?

2. If there is a place of grief in your life right now, imagine God present in it with you. How does He experience your grief?

3. Has your grief ever become a source of destruction in your life? Could the guardrails of taking it to the right place and letting your perspective be transformed keep you in a place of safety?

4. What is the truest gift you have ever received from a time of grieving?

LEFT IN THE DARKNESS

AFTERNOON SUNLIGHT STREAMS UPON THE FACE OF THE WOMAN sitting across from me in the coffee shop. The light dancing in her auburn hair calls out all the gold and amber brown strands, highlighting her beauty. But the light also magnifies the strain around her eyes, the fine wrinkles that are multiplying with every passing year. She is thirty-eight. For twelve years she has been trying to get pregnant. Everything is in place—finances, her readiness to leave her career and stay at home, a patient and tender husband who has endured years of monthly tears, countless tests and fertility strategies. Her parents have quit asking, but they are waiting too. This woman, however, is losing her grip on even wanting her body to carry a baby. Yet to lose it seems like a descent into darkness. Tears form in her eyes, but years of restraint at baby showers and holidays have taught her supreme self-control. "Maybe I'm just mean," she says. "Maybe that's why God won't give me a baby."

I wince. What an impossible reason for God to withhold the blessing of a child. I know this woman—her self-accusation is not true, nor is it the way God works. But she feels herself slipping into darkness and knows no better way to fight.

Amanda, on the other hand, wishes she understood where the darkness came from. For almost a year, nothing in her emotions or even her soul has helped her believe that God was near. It began in July; she and her family were at the beach. She had stayed up after they went to bed; all day she had wanted time by herself to finish her book. The quiet, the sound of the waves outside, and the summer goodness of not having to get up early made late-night reading one of the best parts of vacation time. When she finished the last chapter, she went out to watch the ocean and the stars.

A sense of coldness had been growing in her soul all year, a disconnect between what her head knew was true and what her soul felt. Where had it all started? She wasn't sure. Maybe the year had just been too frazzled; maybe it was her best friend moving away, or her daughter's struggles in school that neither prayer nor appointments with the teacher had remedied. The night sky at the beach had always made God seem so close, so if she sat out on their porch for a while, perhaps she could find the feelings that had accompanied her faith since childhood.

It was a perfect night: rhythmic surf, a clear black sky spangled with stars. But the magic didn't happen. The stretch of night above looked cold and unfriendly. The silence of the stars mocked the message they used to sing to her about God and eternity. She tried to pray; she brought to mind the verses she knew by heart. Nothing happened. Maybe she was just too tired, she thought, so she went to bed. But the next morning, she awoke with that cold, dark place still lodged in her heart. It went on for months. How could she know she was a Christian, how could she even be sure there was a God, if she never felt anything anymore?

At some point in your life, you may have found a darkness growing inside you like the darkness these women experienced. It's a darkness that may have begun in a time of grief or injustice. It may have been provoked by a great sense of shame or guilt. One woman I know was very ill for almost a year. Her body finally recovered, but her spirit didn't. In every situation, one experience is common. We feel unable to believe the way we used to believe. Even if we cling to our faith, there is no joy, no assurance that God is there or that all is well with our soul.

A trap door opens in our heart, and we find ourselves falling to a dark interior place that we did not even know existed. It's not about our grief anymore, or our struggle with our circumstance, or our guilt. It's not about our fears or lack of gratitude. Some observers would diagnose us as depressed, but we are not sure they are right either. Somehow we instinctively know it's about our souls and their connection to God. We realize we cannot pray, sing, believe, theologize, or obey our way out of the darkness into a place of rest. Other people cannot talk or lead us to the light, no matter how much they know or how deeply they care. How do we make our way through this time, which has been called the dark night of the soul, to an expansive and peace-filled heart?

No One Can Help

The first thing we usually do to escape the darkness is to look for help from another person. Our attempt invariably results in failure. Etched in my memory is a late summer night drive down a Texas highway. The grief from my father's death had evolved into a blanket of despair that was no longer just about my father. Again and again I had gone to my husband, trying to explain what I felt, to find answers or at least comfort in his words. But for weeks nothing he said had helped. No matter how he responded, I only ended up more distraught, and he found himself caught between his own grief and his frustration at not being able to help me. That night, in the middle of yet another painful interchange, he pounded the steering wheel and cried out, "Sally, I can't help you!"

My response was more tears. It seemed the only one who could help me had cut the tether that kept me from falling into the abyss of total darkness. We drove on in silence, absorbing the helpless place we found ourselves in. My husband and I share an uncommonly blessed love. If he could not help me, then human help did not exist.

The second thing we try when we are in the dark is to turn on the light for ourselves. We can't do it. A close friend went through a four-year battle, struggling to believe the things about God she had easily believed for over twenty years. A car accident and her first child's departure to college marked the beginning of that time. But it was more than that—a number of prayers had gone unanswered, prayers that seemed important to her and relatively easy for God to take care of. But He didn't. She knew God had the right to answer her prayers however He wished, and yet in His silence she lost all the emotions that had accompanied her faith.

She read the Bible, and nothing happened in her soul for months and months. She examined her life for some issue of grave disobedience and found nothing. Cynicism and disbelief grew, so she spent time trying to praise God for the sake of her heart and time reading books on apologetics for the sake of her mind. She talked to friends; she went to see a counselor. Finally, she just gave up and waited. All her attempts to find her own light only made the darkness darker still.

In times of spiritual darkness, we realize our inadequacy to bring our own soul to a place of rest. No matter how hard we try, the disquiet within only multiplies. John of the Cross understood. His description of soul darkness is five hundred years old, but you may know the truth of his words:

> I will say it plainly: The fire of Love that will afterward unite with the soul and bring it glory is the same fire which begins by assailing it in order to cleanse and purify. . . . [The soul] suffers greatly, wondering if it is

merely abandoned by God to great afflictions. . . .
During this time, as the Spirit prepares the soul for God's
coming in fullness, the fire of God is not bright, but dark
. . . there are times of inner torment and affliction. This is
not at all pleasant, but rather makes the soul believe it is
wandering in an abandoned and arid wasteland. . . . The
soul feels confused in the dark, not knowing what God is
about—or if He is still there at all.[1]

If our own attempts at ending the darkness are so futile,
where can we go to find a gate to rest?

PRESENT IN OUR DARKNESS

The first truth we can cling to when there is no light in our world
or in our hearts is that God is present in our darkness and longs
to comfort us. David sings of God's presence in the darkness in
Psalm 139.

Where can I go from your Spirit?
    Where can I flee from your presence?
If I go up to the heavens, you are there;
    if I make my bed in the depths, you are there. . . .
If I say, "Surely the darkness will hide me
    and the light become night around me,"
even the darkness will not be dark to you;
    the night will shine like the day,
    for darkness is as light to you. (verses 7-8,11-12)

We understand that God would meet us in our grief or fears;
He is a compassionate Father and we are His children. But
David says His tenderness and knowledge of us extend beyond
painful circumstances and explainable events; He is in the darkness with us. To Him it is not night there, yet He endures with

us as we wait out the darkness. Still, the question that plagues us when it is dark is, *How can we know He is here?* The great pain of the darkness is that He will *not* reveal Himself. We feel so alone, so unsure that the personal God we once so easily believed in is still at the center of all.

During a time of great personal darkness I realized that I could not change the heaviness inside me. I accepted the reality that God would probably not show up in a great blaze of glory and rearrange my heart. So I began to pray a very small prayer from one of David's psalms: "Give me a sign of your goodness" (Psalm 86:17). Perhaps if God would show me signs of good, small indications that He was present with me in the nighttime of my soul, then I would be able to endure one day's darkness at a time.

God did. When we are in darkness, God's plan is to comfort us, but He sees far more than we see, and He will choose His own methods and timing to bring that comfort our way. We cannot press Him. But we can pray for signs for good and then for an equal grace, the eyes to see those signs. There is so much we miss in creation, in the turn of events, in a choice phrase we read, or in a small kindness from a friend. If we look, if we take time, if we listen, there will be pinpoints of light within the darkness. We will experience those intersection moments when we realize that God is present in our darkness and longs to meet us there.

Just such a time occurred one cold spring morning when I was out for a walk. My destination when I needed to think was the reservoir near our home. A bike path along the river led to the dam that held the reservoir in place. The darkness within me was heavy, just as it had been for months. But as I made my way on the walkway across the dam, I saw something I had never seen before. Hundreds of swallows filled the air over the reservoir. I stopped and leaned against the railing that separated the pedestrian path from the edge of the dam and watched.

In great swooping motions they descended close to the dam where I stood, crisscrossing each other's paths in an elaborate configuration of dance. Then as if bidding some call I could not hear, they scattered, flying up and away. But before they were out of sight, they returned, some flying high, some low as they wove intricate patterns of flight. Again and again they did this: the swooping weaving beside me, the scattering, the regathering. For more than fifteen minutes I watched, transfixed. Their Creator was calling out the movements of their dance. They were responding. Nothing spoke of randomness; all spoke of design.

My darkness was like that. Their Creator was also my Creator, orchestrating the rhythms of my soul. When He was ready, the darkness would begin to break. In the meantime, He was in it beside me.

AT WORK IN DARKNESS

Second, in our times of darkness we need to take heart. As surprising as it is to us, the wellspring of God's creativity is hidden within darkness. God fashioned the world in the midst of a creation shrouded by darkness. David reminds us that our physical bodies were formed within the darkness of our mother's womb: "... when I was made in the secret place. When I was woven together in the depths of the earth" (Psalm 139:15). The plant world, the animal kingdom, the wombs of women all bear witness to the same principle: God grows life under the covering of darkness. This especially holds true in the realm of our soul. The remaking of our heart to be like Jesus is not a process we manage or can even observe. Mystery cradles what God is about. Like a sculptor who keeps his work from public eye until the great unveiling, so God often cloaks the work He is doing in us.

For instance, the soul darkness we experience is meant to take us to deep places. In our darkness, God intends that we become painfully aware of our inadequacies and failures, and that we come face to face with His unfailing love. Asaph expressed the wonder of the God who meets us with tender mercies when we realize the darkness is not just around us but also deeply within us:

> When my heart was grieved
>   and my spirit embittered,
> I was senseless and ignorant;
>   I was a brute beast before you.
> Yet I am always with you;
>   you hold me by my right hand.
> You guide me with your counsel,
>   and afterward you take me into glory. (Psalm 73:21-24)

In the darkness we see the ugliness embedded in our hearts. But we also have the opportunity to come face to face with the powerful, lovely grace of God. He remade Asaph's heart in the midst of darkness.

There are places in our hearts, broad places of rest and fullness, that cannot exist unless we live through periods of darkness. In the darkness we can be assured that God will be our Comforter in His way and His time, and we can be sure that He is at work to make something beautiful of our souls. The question is, while He is doing His work, how do we live through it?

GOD'S CALL IN THE MIDST OF THE DARKNESS

DON'T RUSH THE DARKNESS

The author of Lamentations described the galling bitterness and disorientation he experienced during a bleak time. He counsels us simply to endure through it.

> It is good to wait quietly
>   for the salvation of the LORD.
> It is good for a man to bear the yoke
>   while he is young.

Let him sit alone in silence,
  for the LORD has laid it on him.
Let him bury his face in the dust—
  there may yet be hope.
Let him offer his cheek to one who would strike him,
  and let him be filled with disgrace. (Lamentations 3:26-30)

There are things in our souls we cannot fix. We can refrain from sin—God makes that very clear in His Word—but we cannot always reshape our hearts to sing a different song. Sometimes we just have to wait.

Beth's soul is beginning to heal, but only after several years of letting the pain of her life come to the surface. Before the darkness descended, she had managed her soul by efficiency and success. Her freelance career as a graphic designer in a healthy economy meant that plenty of work and all the applause that goes with success came her way. Her friends never attempted to plumb the depths of her soul; they were too impressed with her business ability, her leadership in a large community Bible study, her exercise program, and her fabulous vacations. It was just as well. There was a lot she preferred to keep hidden in the darkness: her past promiscuity, the marriage and quick divorce of her late teens, the alcohol she turned to so often for relief.

But God had other plans. Her Bible study chose John's gospel for its fall curriculum. As they came to John 11, the death and raising of Lazarus, Beth's private past erupted with volcanic vengeance. She was Lazarus, called back from the grave. But she did not know how to rid herself of the grave clothes. Martha's warning in the story, "But Lord, by this time there is a bad odor," put a knife through Beth's soul. She knew she was a Christian, but how could she ever be cleansed from all the darkness she had stashed so deep in her heart?

In an attempt to deal with what she was uncovering, Beth did a most uncharacteristic thing. She let the smell of all she'd done roll over her soul. She pulled back from her endless cycle of doing. She took walks in the early morning and got out her easel and oil paints. She sat down in the afternoon with a cup of tea to read and think. Her business suffered; her calendar didn't run over with engagements. In her words, she chose to wait in the darkness, praying that God Himself would remove the grave clothes.

LIVE IN THE DARKNESS

Beth's decision to let her secrets take her into darkness was only the beginning. If the darkness is to do its good work in us, we must also be willing to live in it for awhile. In our Western culture, we have grown accustomed to a Christianity of techniques. Therefore, it is easy to read the words "don't rush the darkness" and think this is something we do in order to manage the darkness so we can quickly move past it to a place of rest. The truth is, we are also called to submit to the dark night of our soul as the place where God would have us be. In God's time He ends darkness. The Scriptures promise with authority that "weeping may remain for a night, but rejoicing comes in the morning" (Psalm 30:5). But before God brings morning to our souls, He calls us to wait patiently in the darkness, not to find a quick way out of it.

As I write these words, I think of a couple whose daughter almost died from anorexia nervosa. Like most parents, as the problem came into focus for them, they explored every possible strategy for helping their child: reason, control, non-control, counseling, a therapeutic residency program. But still their daughter, impervious to their love, impervious to her own declining health, continued to lose weight. Slowly the realization dawned. Until God chose to lift this darkness, they would have to learn to make their life in the midst of it.

Over several years, a beautiful detachment grew in their souls, not the detachment of not caring, but the detachment of gentleness. They would continue to choose to believe that Jesus was with them and their daughter in this darkness that seemed to have no coming dawn. All their fear, anger, love, and hurt they would give to God. They would learn, as the writer of Lamentations advised, to wait in silence.

Whether our darkness arises from painful circumstances or the weather of our own souls, the only gate to rest is choosing to live in and through it, choosing to receive the darkness as a gift. My husband and I went through a time of profound spiritual upheaval a number of years ago. We could not trace our feelings to circumstances; God appeared to have moved far from us without cause. The Bible was lifeless; the memories of how it had spoken to us in the past mocked our present longings. We prayed. We kept reading Scripture. We waited for signs of good. We wondered what we had done wrong. We doubted if our past experiences of God's presence had even been real— perhaps we had made it all up. We were sure we would never know His nearness again. The heaviness in our souls appeared to have no remedy.

One windy March day in the midst of this darkness, we went for a long walk. We walked and prayed. We stooped and sat on the brown grass of early spring and prayed. The wind blew. The heavens were empty. All we could discern were the quiet words from Psalm 46: "Be still, and know that I am God." But no release came from these words. There was only the emptiness and the command to live in that emptiness until God filled it.

In His time, God slowly began to mend our souls. But it was His time. In the meantime, all we could do was wait. There are no shortcuts.

RESIST THE TEMPTATION

As we wait in the darkness, we must resist the temptation to dispel it by lighting our own fires. The prophet Isaiah warns us of the danger of fire lighting.

Who among you fears the LORD
  and obeys the word of his servant?
Let him who walks in the dark,
  who has no light,
trust in the name of the LORD
  and rely on his God.
But now all you who light fires
  and provide yourselves with flaming torches,
go, walk in the light of your fires
  and of the torches you have set ablaze.
This is what you shall receive from my own hand:
  You will lie down in torment. (Isaiah 50:10-11)

Jesus Himself is the supreme example of one who did not light His own fires to banish the darkness. In the wilderness, as weakened as He was by forty days of fasting, He resisted Satan's solutions to hunger, human misunderstanding, and the coming pain of the cross. Later in His ministry, He refused to call down fire from heaven on the unbelieving. He allowed His glory to be veiled. He spent His life among disciples who did not understand Him. Finally, on the cross, He would not call for angels to spare Him and destroy those who were crucifying Him. At every turn He submitted to the narrow way of darkness.

In our dark times, we too are tempted. Distractions, busyness, addictions to ease our hurting hearts, control to manage chaos, success to bolster our egos—all these things promise a quicker exit from the darkness. We need to hear Isaiah's warning: these alternatives never open the gate to rest; they will lead only to torment in our souls.

What Will the Darkness Bring?

I will give you the treasures of darkness,
  riches stored in secret places,

so that you may know that I am the LORD,
    the God of Israel, who summons you by name.
(Isaiah 45:3)

TREASURE

Is the darkness worth it? Isaiah spoke of "the treasures of darkness" that God would give to the Persian king Cyrus as Cyrus
returned the exiled Jews to their homeland. We do not know for
certain what Isaiah was alluding to, but his words call forth a
powerful image. Treasures abound in the darkness. Seeds come
to life in unlit places underground. Costly jewel stones lie
embedded in the dark interiors of ordinary rocks. Oil and gas
reserves run far beneath the earth's surface. The dark depths of
the ocean teem with life. The natural world draws pictures so
that we might understand the spiritual world; the darkness holds
great treasure.

Yet it is often only after the darkness has passed that we recognize the precious things God gave us during the nighttime of
our soul. A friend whose marriage broke down during an agonizing five years of unfaithfulness and broken promises said to me
recently, "I wish I wasn't divorced. But God became so real to me
in those five hard years that if still being married meant I would
also lose all I've gained with Jesus, I could not make the trade."

In C. S. Lewis's story *The Horse and His Boy*, a boy named
Shasta feels his whole life has been a hurtful journey.
Abandoned at birth and raised by a merciless fisherman, Shasta
determines to run away and find a better life. Several times in his
journey, frightening lions pursue him. The lions epitomize for
him the fearful difficulties of his life. As his flight to safety
reaches a dangerous pitch, Shasta realizes he is once again being
pursued by something he cannot see. Terror and self-pity almost
undo him, but then the thing pursuing him makes a startling
request: Tell me your sorrows. Shasta pours out all the danger,
the loneliness, and the injustices of his life. He explains how

horrible his encounters with the dreadful lions have been. Lewis continues the dialogue between these two as this unknown being makes himself known to Shasta.

> "I do not call you unfortunate. . . . I was the lion who forced you to join with Aravis. I was the cat who confronted you among the houses of the dead. I was the lion who drove the jackals from you while you slept. I was the lion who gave the Horses the new strength of fear for the last mile so that you should reach King Lune in time. And I was the lion you do not remember who pushed the boat in which you lay, a child near death, so that it came to shore where a man sat, wakeful at night to receive you."
>
> "Who are you?" asked Shasta.
>
> "Myself," said the Voice, very deep and low so that the earth shook: and again, "Myself," loud and clear and gay: and then the third time, "Myself," whispered so softly you could hardly hear it, and yet it seemed to come from all round you as if the leaves rustled with it.[2]

Myself, myself, myself, the Voice replies. Lewis's words are only story, but they are a gate to understanding as well. The Triune God waits in the darkness with us, for us. There, as in no other place, He gives us the gift of Himself.

STRENGTH

There is also a strengthening that comes to our soul as we learn to endure the deprivations and fears the darkness brings. Plants need their full measure of darkness; in excessive light, they grow too fast and become spindly. Similarly, darkness tempers our lives with strength. Carlo Carretto says,

> To reach the "night of the senses"—the time when we become rulers of our passions and are able to resist the

extravagances of our taste and physical pleasure—that takes some fasting!

But this is nothing yet. This is only the beginning—baby stuff, you might say.

There is more to come!

There is another darker, much more painful night.

It is the "night of the soul," the night in which we chatterboxes have to learn to keep still.

We who are so ready to ask for things—now we shall not dare to ask.

We fall silent, thunderstruck with the grandeur that confronts us: God.

The dark night of the spirit is the mature ability of the human being to love God in the dark, to accept the design even without seeing it, to bear the distance without complaining, even when love thrusts us toward him until we writhe with longing.[3]

HOPE

Finally, the darkness is meant to open a door to hope for us. As we accept its presence with us, as we submit to staying in it until God removes it, and as we refuse the temptation to light our own fires, God grows within us the capacity to live out of a spacious heart. Without the darkness, our souls are cramped. We are confined by our fears, guilt, and shame. We are limited by our weaknesses and vulnerable to new sinful choices. We are dependent on our sense of our soul's well-being.

The amazing truth is that the darkness doesn't just "happen" to us; God calls us into it. He waits with us there, and He leads us through it to give us a new life. In Hosea 2 God uses the word *desert* instead of *darkness*, but God's work there is the same:

"Therefore I am now going to allure her;
    I will lead her into the desert and speak tenderly to her.

There I will give her back her vineyards,
    and will make the Valley of Achor a door of hope.
There she will sing as in the days of her youth,
    as in the day she came up out of Egypt." (Hosea 2:14-15)

God made this promise to His estranged people by referring to a shameful moment in their history. On the threshold of their entrance into the Promised Land, after the miraculous crossing of the Jordan and the mighty display of God's power at Jericho, a man named Achan chose to disobey God. His sin brought serious consequences to the entire nation. The Israelites faltered in what should have been an easy battle, and the people lost courage.

When Joshua, the Israelite leader, discovered that Achan's sin had caused the defeat, he gathered the nation around this man and his family to execute God's judgment. Achan, his children, and all their possessions were stoned and burned. Rocks were piled on the charred heap. The Israelites named this place of God's judgment the Valley of Achor, which means "the place of trouble." It marked the fact that even on the cusp of enjoying God's goodness, people would still foul the waters of His grace.

But Hosea declared that Achor, the place of loss and death and reproach, was the very place where God held out His love. He is the One who draws us into the desert-dark place, but in that barren environment His mercy will take root in us, and a door of hope will open. In the darkness and through it, we will find rest for our souls.

Taking Time

1. Have you ever been through a time you would call the "dark night of the soul"?

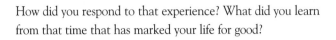

How did you respond to that experience? What did you learn
from that time that has marked your life for good?

2. If you are presently enduring a time of darkness, sit with your
own heart before God.

How were you led into this desert?

Have you made efforts to turn on your own light?

What would it mean to choose to simply live in it, to wait on
God, to let Him be with you in the dark?

FORGING A
PLACE OF REST

*Let us, therefore, make every effort to enter that rest,
so that no one will fall by following [the Israelites']
example of disobedience.*

HEBREWS 4:11

As OUR FIRST PARENTS WERE DRIVEN FROM THEIR HOME IN EDEN,
cherubim and a flaming sword blocked the gate back to that garden. Now a new rest is available because of Jesus Christ, but the
difficulties that arise in our souls and our circumstances block us
so that we often find it impossible to live out of a quiet and spacious heart. It is true that feelings and circumstances can be
overwhelming. But rest does not come after a long battle in
which we manage to change or to conquer all the issues that
keep our hearts in turmoil. Life will never be solved this side of
heaven, so it's good to know that the heart rest God desires to
give us is located in the midst of these very difficulties. In fact,
the surprising glory of our struggles is that they offer a gate to a
rest far richer and truer than we have ever known before.

But in order to pass through that gate, we need to deal with
more than just heart turbulence. We can approach the things

we've talked about in chapters 2 through 7 with a courageous determination to face the reality in our hearts. We can long to see our issues transformed into gates to God's garden. And we can still fall short of entering through the gates. Two other obstacles block our way: the pace of our world and a deep fear of rest itself.

RESISTING REST IS NATURAL

TRAPPED BY THE PACE

We must be honest about the constant press of our Western world. Our culture does not want us to stop, to be quiet, to listen. If we are to enter into rest, we must learn to resist its demands. Obviously, the primary purpose of this book has not been to speak to the choices we must make or the strategies we must adopt so that room exists in our daily life for true heart rest to grow. At the same time, we must face reality: we will never know an internal place of intimate connection with God unless we develop the discipline of actually making space in our schedule for "Sabbath" times, times like those God Himself enjoys.

Rest is not a magic kingdom that will instantly grow within us just because we long for it or even pray about it. We must set apart chunks of time—time for quiet, for relationship, for celebrating what is. In the midst of a world that harasses us with calls to endless busyness, we have to make the decision to cultivate peace of heart; it will not descend upon us.

Stopping this world is almost impossible. Women tell me stories of life as it was just twenty years ago when they were growing up. One woman related that her father served on two community boards as well as his church leadership board. He owned his own business, but somehow he managed to be home by 6:30. On Sundays he spent the afternoon playing games with his children: board games by a fire in the winter, ball in the back yard with all the neighborhood children when the weather was warmer.

Another woman (one of eight children) had a university professor for a father. Wanting to protect their family life, he insisted
that none of his children would participate in weeknight activities. Somehow, it worked. These eight children involved themselves in sports, afternoon music lessons, school clubs; but they
understood the parameters: quiet evenings and family.

Another family in more recent years took the profit made
from the sale of a successful business and bought a tract of land.
They homeschool while the father manages his affairs from
home. A nearby city is available when they want it, but determination and the finances to choose their own lifestyle have
built a firm wall against demands from the outside.

Can we slow our lives down and make them look like these
families'? Our culture seems to insist on much higher involvement than did the worlds of the first two women above. As for
the third family, its strategy requires a financial freedom few of
us have.

Again, this is not a book about choosing simplicity or chart-
ing out Sabbath-rest time on our calendars. But there is no way
to think about rest without affirming that rest is not just an atti-
tude of the heart. We cannot keep up the ever-increasing pace
of our lives and expect to be people of rest. What our hearts
prize, our lives will express. The converse is just as true: what our
lives fail to embrace, our hearts will never know.

Unless we disengage and enter rest with our actions and
choices as well as our minds, we do not really value it. Rest
means to stop, to celebrate, to allow ourselves to suffer lack. In
resting we pull away from doing although all is not done. But our
culture only knows a mutated form of rest. When all our accomplishing crashes into the wall of utter fatigue, we finally take a
break and call that "rest."

Perhaps we can see the difference between God's true rest and
our "rest" by considering the difference between the words *recreation* and *amusement*. Embedded in the root words for recreation

and amusement are vastly different concepts. *Recreation* is the state of being *re-created*. It is something we do or choose that fills our soul and body so that we are stronger and richer as a result. Recreation nurtures us. *Amusement,* on the other hand, literally means "to not think." When we choose amusement we shut down, we disengage. Even more pointed is the ancient meaning of amusement: "to deceive." Could it be that we are deceived when we think that the answer to our weariness is amusement, not recreation? Life is not meant to alternate spasmodically between exhausting, frantic activity and mindless states where we have no energy for anything. We must learn to say no to relentless schedules and cultivate places in our lives for true recreation. Only we can make the choices for what refurbishes our souls and our relationships.

AFRAID OF THE SILENCE

Learning to choose rest in the midst of our culture is more than a battle with the world around us. The pace we live with has constricted our souls as well as our schedules. Because we have learned to define ourselves by what we do, the answer to the question "Did you have a good day?" hinges on whether we were able to mark many or few things off of our to-do list. We believe effective, successful people have at least seven good habits, and they work them all the time. Who are we if we stop? Nobody. But if we are to enter rest, a shift must take place inside our souls.

Yet many of us don't believe it. We are convinced that we cannot resist the pace forced upon us. Blaming our inability on impossible circumstances, we promise ourselves that just around the next corner, life will settle down and we will slow down. But it rarely happens. Why? I believe we are afraid of being alone, afraid of blocks of time when we have nothing we have to do. If rest means entering a space of fearful emptiness, many of us are not sure we want to go there. We may be exhausted, but we'll find something besides rest to fill our fatigue: a video, a nap, a long phone call with a friend. Obviously, these things are not "wrong," but we need to face our own hearts.

We are afraid to choose rest because we are afraid of silence, afraid of what we might hear if all sounds were to cease. I know this full well. We lived for seven years in the foothills of the Canadian Rockies. An hour's drive from our city was a small retreat center established by a couple who understood the need we all have for space and time away from the routine of life. The center contained everything a woman like myself might dream of: private bedrooms, real baths, nutritious, homemade food, a well-stocked library with a huge fireplace. The surrounding property fed the soul as well with a swift, glacier-sourced river, hiking trails, and prayer and meditation paths for times of quiet. I looked forward to time there with my husband and in the quiet company of others.

But the facility included one place where I did not want to stay. A small private cabin stood in a grove of trees on the other side of the river, connected to life at the retreat center by a swinging footbridge. The furnishings were stark: a miniature wood-burning stove, a lantern, a latrine, a twin bed, a small desk and chair, a tiny front porch with a single chair. It was a perfect place to fast, to pray, to sleep, to read. On one occasion when my husband and I were staying in the lodge, the cabin was empty, and he wanted me to see it. Having used this cabin himself, he was urging me to take a few days for a private retreat. He had every reason to believe I needed it. Five children, many overnight guests, the constant press of making meals, my teaching ministry, and never-ending housework made for industrial-size responsibilities. He was committed to helping me find time alone.

But as we stood in that little cabin and I leafed through the guest book where the people who had stayed there had written their names, the dates of their stay, and any reflections they wanted to share, my first thought was, "I am *not* coming here." It was too alone, too quiet, too frightening. A weekend away with girlfriends—that sounded like fun. Three days at the retreat lodge, reading, hiking, sitting by the fire with my husband—that sounded like heaven. But total aloneness? That was a different matter.

I knew intuitively what I was afraid of. What might I hear if all around me were totally at rest? In the silence of fasting, sleeping, and awaking to no one and nothing-that-had-to-be-done, what might I learn? It was too overwhelmingly unknown. I wanted some silence, some rest in my life; but I wanted it in small, manageable chunks. I did not want to give rest too much time to talk to me.

In view of all that opposes us, both within and without, we must deliberately pursue rest of heart. Every one of us faces challenging issues of the heart, pressure from our culture, and our own fear of silence. To help you dare to push past whatever opposes you, I want to give you a vision for the garden that awaits you on the other side of the gate.

A WALK THROUGH FOUR GARDENS

The Bible depicts four gardens, and all of them can tell us something about the garden rest we can taste even here and now. Life in this world began in a garden, and in that place Adam and Eve experienced all the goodness that we call rest. Today our longings are only met in part, but they will find their everlasting fulfillment as we enter that eternal city that Revelation speaks of. At the center of that city is a garden with a river flowing through it. But Eden and eternity are not the only gardens of Scripture. As the Bible tells the story of God's redemptive love, two other gardens come into view. Together these four gardens will give us a clearer picture of what our hearts were made for. They will help us fight the pressures of our culture and our fears of rest.

THE GARDEN AT EDEN
Rest is richness. The first thing we learn from the garden at Eden is that true rest fills up the deepest longings of our heart. We are

afraid to step away from our culture's pace because we might miss out; we are afraid to be still because what we might hear in the silence could be terrifying. But our fears are far from God's reality. Rest will never diminish our souls or give us only a pauper's fare when we desire so much more. The wise writer of Ecclesiastes understood our hearts when he said, "The eye never has enough of seeing, nor the ear its fill of hearing" (Ecclesiastes 1:8). The pull our culture exerts on us touches these longings; we sense in our souls a never-ending hunger for something more, something new.

The bounty God placed in His creation meets that hunger. One cannot read the Genesis account or consider the planet on which God placed us without realizing how crammed it is with so many different things to hear, see, touch, smell, taste, experience. God designed this earth to speak to our longings for beauty and delight. The great oceans of our world that hint at eternity, plants and trees in all their variety of abundance, a sun to rule the day and stars set in the expanse of the heavens—all these are only the beginning of God's amazing creativity. Genesis speaks of so much more: the water teeming with living creatures, the birds flying above the earth in the expanse of the sky, the wild animals, the livestock, the creeping creatures living close to the earth.

In the midst of His overflowing creation, God fashioned His piece de resistance, a garden. He planted it in the east and gave it to Adam as his home. Just as the larger creation revealed God's goodness, so did the garden. The trees there were pleasing to the eye and good for food. A river that flowed from the garden was powerful enough to be the headwaters for four major rivers that blessed the entire region. Gold, pearls, and onyx were found in the surrounding countryside; like a setting for a beautiful ring, they showed off the greatest jewel of all, the garden. Through the physical gift of that garden set in the midst of an equally splendid creation, we catch glimpses of the Creator who can fill not only an earth but also our very souls with richness.

Our understanding of rest misses so much of what God made available in the garden. It's not just the remembered legalism of the Pharisees or the practices of certain Christian groups that turn rest into less. We do it as well. Because our souls have been out of joint (as well as sinful and flawed) since the Fall, we see rest as restrictive; we are convinced it means denial rather than an entering into beauty and richness. But we are wrong.

Rest flows into work. The garden at Eden not only teaches us that rest is richness; it also explains for us the interplay between rest and work. The compulsive doing that permeates our culture creates fear within us by setting up a black-and-white dichotomy: achieve and be somebody, or give in to the emptiness of "rest" and lose your identity and purpose. But God's rest does not preclude work. God intended that Adam and Eve shape His world with a creative intensity that mirrored His own. The work He had for them, however, was meant to flow out of rest. This truth comes into focus when we realize that the Genesis concept of a *day* is opposite to our view. We believe the day begins with the blare of our alarm clock. Early morning marks the starting place, and we rush forward from that point, pushing until we reach our goal, the end of the day and the chance to finally relax. Our rest is a reward for our work.

But in the beginning, God saw this world's time from a different perspective. As God defined the word *day*, He called it *evening and morning*. The garden pulsed with opportunities for meaningful work, but it was to be work energized by true rest.

Equally important, the rest that flowed into work found its source in relationship. We know from Genesis 3:8 that the Lord God walked in the garden "in the cool of the day." Evening was Adam and Eve's time of deep connection with their Creator-Friend. Did the conversations enriching that time together shape the form and meaning of the next morning's work? Did the quiet of that time together restore their hearts and renew their bodies so they were ready for dawn's light?

Rest flows out of a pure heart. Finally, from that first garden we discover that rest flows out of hearts that carry no burden of shame and have no need to hide. I was afraid of rest because I knew it meant embracing silence. I feared that silence would expose my heart and introduce me to a terrifying loneliness. Before they ate from the forbidden tree, Adam and Eve knew the rest of being free from all shame and they knew the piercing sweetness of intimacy with each other and with God. But they destroyed the very thing that fed their souls, then established destructive patterns of self-protection in their last hours in that garden. After their fatal encounter with the serpent, Adam and Eve were too busy designing their fig leaves, too busy avoiding God, too busy blaming one another to know rest of heart and the intimacy it brings. It is the same for us. Our attempts to cover and manage our guilt and shame and our fear of what silence might say to us about ourselves drive us from rest.

The rest of the garden at Eden is the rest our souls were made for. We still long for that rest, for a place of beauty and variety. We long for a place where our labor flows from the headwaters of deep soul peace and contentment. We wish we knew for sure that our work was meaningful and pleased God's heart. And we wish with all our hearts that we had nothing to hide, so that all the posturing we do could be put to bed, forever. Those longings exist because the garden was real and we were made for it.

THE GARDEN AT GETHSEMANE

> Then Jesus went with his disciples to a place called Gethsemane, and he said to them, "Sit here while I go over there and pray." He took Peter and the two sons of Zebedee along with him, and he began to be sorrowful and troubled. Then he said to them, "My soul is overwhelmed with sorrow to the point of death. Stay here and keep watch with me."

Going a little farther, he fell with his face to the ground and prayed, "My Father, if it is possible, may this cup be taken from me. Yet not as I will, but as you will."

Then he returned to his disciples and found them sleeping. "Could you men not keep watch with me for one hour?" he asked Peter. . . .

He went away a second time and prayed, "My Father, if it is not possible for this cup to be taken away unless I drink it, may your will be done."

When he came back, he again found them sleeping, because their eyes were heavy. So he left them and went away once more and prayed the third time, saying the same thing.

Then he returned to the disciples and said to them, "Are you still sleeping and resting? Look, the hour is near, and the Son of Man is betrayed into the hands of sinners. Rise, let us go! Here comes my betrayer!" (Matthew 26:36-40,42-46)

In order to undo what we all did in Adam, the scene moves to a second garden—Gethsemane, the place of dying. Christ has entered this garden first. As we see Him there, agonizing in prayer, we realize how difficult it was, even for the Son of God Himself, to embrace this garden of death. He chose Gethsemane with the hurt of Judas's coming betrayal pressing against His soul. He walked into it knowing that, for the most part, those who loved Him would not be adequate to stand with Him in His dying.

We ask ourselves, *How can anything be learned about rest from this garden? What rest can there be in dying?* For Jesus, the rest lay in letting go of every prerogative, every privilege. He saw past the shame of death on the cross to a future joy. As He died, He was able to say, "It is finished" (John 19:30). And it was totally finished. His death removed God's judgment from us and gave us the very thing God had longed to give us since we were shut out of the first garden — the opportunity for intimacy with the Father and the possibility of having our hearts deeply changed.

Isaiah in his own time looked ahead to Christ's death and said, "After the suffering of his soul, he will see the light of life and be satisfied" (Isaiah 53:11). Jesus said dying was the necessary prelude to real life. As His crucifixion drew near, He used a garden metaphor to explain that when we resist dying, we also avoid life: "I tell you the truth, unless a kernel of wheat falls to the ground and dies, it remains only a single seed. But if it dies, it produces many seeds" (John 12: 24). So the rest in dying is one that sees beyond the present moment to the life that the dying will usher in. Jesus lived His whole life in this reality. Rest demands a dying, for dying is the unavoidable gate to life.

But what does this dying look like for us? Without a doubt, it means dying to our expectations, dreams, assumptions, and strivings about what life should be. It means we choose to *suffer lack*. There is a great dying in admitting that some things will never be. Perhaps our alcoholic child will never choose sobriety, no matter how many years go by. Perhaps our body will never quit hurting. Perhaps all the effort in the world will never achieve the financial security we have tried so hard to provide. Ultimately, our dying is a faint mirror of Jesus' dying. We have to submit to the sovereign hand of God. Life does not always go the way we hoped it would. We grieve; for a time we may rail against outcomes we can't change, but there is no rest until we embrace the life we have been given. A resignation full of sighs, a grudging acceptance tinged with cynicism and bitterness, a mourning that never ends are not the dying to which we are called. God asks us to let go on a much more profound level.

In that letting go, our hearts learn to make two confessions. First, God is God and we are not. In Psalm 50, as God rebukes both the religious and the wicked, He makes a statement that cuts to every heart: "You thought I was altogether like you. But

I will rebuke you and accuse you to your face." Our dying means we admit we are not God; we are not in control. The great restlessness in our souls will find no end as long as we continue to push against the goads, determined to cling to the belief that by enough effort we will produce the life we long for.

Connected to that confession is the second one. We must accept that we are very, very human. We are fallen, frail, ephemeral. This second garden teaches us that we must die to our posturing about who we really are. God identified Moses as the most humble man who ever lived, and He declared that Moses shared a face-to-face friendship with Him as no other person ever had (Numbers 12:3; Deuteronomy 34:10). Moses was able to enter into that sort of intimacy with God because he so fully embraced the limitations of what it means to be human. Such an acceptance does not come easily. Yet in Eugene Peterson's paraphrase of Psalm 90, a psalm Moses wrote, we see a man at rest; he has admitted the reality of his own humanity. In doing so, he has found his home, his place of rest, in the love of God:

> God, it seems you've been our home forever;
>   long before the mountains were born,
> Long before you brought earth itself to birth,
>   from "once upon a time" to "kingdom come" —you are
>   God. . . .
>
> Your anger is far and away too much for us;
>   we're at the end of our rope. . . .
> We live for seventy years or so
>   (with luck we might make it to eighty),
> And what do we have to show for it? Trouble.
>   Toil and trouble and a marker in the graveyard.
> Who can make sense of such rage,
>   such anger against the very ones who fear you?

Oh! Teach us to live well! . . .
Come back, God—how long do we have to wait?—
    and treat your servants with kindness for a change. . . .
Let your servants see what you're best at—
    the ways you rule and bless your children.
And let the loveliness of our Lord, our God, rest on us,
    confirming the work that we do.
    Oh, yes. Affirm the work that we do! (MSG)

Moses died many times over to false perceptions we often have of ourselves—the illusions that we can be good enough on our own to stand before God, that we can fend off our mortality, that we can make our life meaningful and important by our own effort. In that dying he found rest; he found a home; he found that God alone was far better than Moses at ruling and blessing the world. It is a dying to admit our frailty and our fallenness, just as it is a dying to admit that God alone is God and has the right to do as He pleases in His creation and in our lives. But it is a dying God calls us to embrace.

Our culture demands that we strive and stress our way through life; as we learn to embrace the garden at Gethsemane, the internal chains that bind us to our culture die as well. And in speaking the truth about our own hearts, that we are fragile and fallen and flawed, we die to our need to pretend. In the nighttime place of giving up what this second garden demands, we find Jesus there with us. He never falls asleep in prayer. He prays with us and for us that we might drink the cup of our own dying.

THE GARDEN OF EASTER DAWN

But the second garden is not the end. Scripture's third garden takes us to a new place. Friends placed Christ's body in a tomb in that third garden, but this place that cradled the dead Christ became the place of resurrection. In this garden, the indestructible life of Jesus Christ overcame all grief, all dying. The world is familiar with dying, but it knows little of a death that leads to hope. All sorts of things in our world end in ugly and tragic deaths. Relationships, plans, people, and dreams all die unjustly, prematurely, irrevocably. The response to much of this dying is predictable. We resort to cynicism; we devise vows and schemes to protect ourselves from the pain of future dyings. In the process, our hearts are filled with apathy, anger, and unhealed sorrows. But the third garden stands in the midst of that river of despair and points to the risen Christ.

More than just a garden where life triumphs over death in a general and cosmic sense, this third garden is a place where one by one, name by name, we are called to enter into Resurrection life.

> Mary stood outside the tomb crying. As she wept, she bent over to look into the tomb and saw two angels in white, seated where Jesus' body had been. . . .
>
> They asked her, "Woman, why are you crying?"
>
> "They have taken my Lord away," she said, "and I don't know where they have put him." At this, she turned around and saw Jesus standing there, but she did not realize that it was Jesus.
>
> "Woman," he said, "why are you crying? Who is it you are looking for?"
>
> Thinking he was the gardener, she said, "Sir, if you have carried him away, tell me where you have put him, and I will get him."
>
> Jesus said to her, "Mary."
>
> She turned toward him and cried out in Aramaic, "Rabboni!" (which means Teacher). (John 20:11,13-16)

"Mary," Jesus said as she met Him in the garden that first Easter morning, still in her grief, still not seeing Him for who He was. *Mary.* He called her by name to see and embrace the gladness of His resurrection. In that garden, Christ's heart was filled with the names of the others He loved. As soon as Mary realized it was Jesus, He had a message for her to deliver: "Do not hold on to me, for I have not yet returned to the Father. Go instead to my brothers and tell them, 'I am returning to my Father and your Father, to my God and your God.'" He wanted each one of His friends—friends He now for the first time called His brothers—to know that death had been swallowed up in life.

Our own hearts know they cannot rest if the ending is still up for grabs. It is hard to let go and trust unless we have confidence that someone of immense wisdom, power, and love is directing the outcome of all things. Our need for assurance that all will be well pulls at our heart. The Resurrection garden shouts at us, "All will be well!" In that assurance our hearts can find rest. Julian of Norwich, a Christian from the fourteenth century, understood the immensity of all that God made right through Jesus:

> Do not be troubled. You will see for yourself that all manner of things will be well. . . . Just as God was so powerful He made everything from nothing, in the same way He will make everything well that is not well.[1]

THE GARDEN IN THE MIDST OF THE CITY

> I saw the Holy City, the new Jerusalem, coming down out of heaven from God. . . . And I heard a loud voice from the throne saying, "Now the dwelling of God is with men, and he will live with them. They will be his people, and God himself will be with them and be their God. . . . "
>
> I did not see a temple in the city, because the Lord God Almighty and the Lamb are its temple. . . .
>
> Then the angel showed me the river of the water of life, as clear as crystal, flowing from the throne of God and of the Lamb down the middle of the great street of

the city. On each side of the river stood the tree of life, bearing twelve crops of fruit. . . . And the leaves of the tree are for the healing of the nations. No longer will there be any curse. . . .

"These words are trustworthy and true." (Revelation 21:2-3,22; 22:1-3,6)

The fourth and final garden in Scripture opens wide the gate to rest. It is the garden we spoke of in chapter 1, the garden in the midst of a city. As the story of God's love affair with this world moves to its final two chapters in the book of Revelation, the writer paints a picture of the New Jerusalem, the heavenly city. The writer lays out the dimensions of the city and the materials from which it will be built. It is a costly, exquisite place whose beauty defies human description. But it is not just a city, for at its heart is a garden where the tree of life is planted, the very tree that God withheld from man after Adam chose to eat from the tree of the knowledge of good and evil. A river flowing from the throne of God nourishes that tree so that it faithfully produces a variety of fruits and so that its leaves can bring healing. From that garden-center at the heart of the eternal city, the rich life of God flows out to enrich and bless the city's inhabitants. No curse, no darkness blight this place. The people of this city have deep purpose; they serve their King. They see Him face to face; they belong to Him. His very name is written across their countenance.

That city with its river-garden center paints a picture for us that is meant to shape our present. Rest is a life sourced in the life of God. The garden at Eden will not be restored. God's final destination for us is a city, a place of community and connection, not a place of isolation or retreat. Whether we live in suburbs or cities, most of us live surrounded by people and activity. Much of it is inescapable, simply part of what it means to be human. But in the midst of all the doing of our lives, God intends that we be people who live out of a garden heart, a garden made beautiful by the river of living water that flows through it. Jesus Christ Himself promised that it could be this way: "Whoever believes in me, as the Scripture has said, streams of living water will flow from within him" (John 7:38). Just as the river of life flows from the throne of God to nurture that heavenly garden, so the living water of the Holy Spirit is meant to flow to the garden of our hearts. As that water cleanses and feeds the core of our being, we will know rest.

So how do we find rest, that broad and expansive place where our hearts can just be? Where is that place where rich solitude rides on a current of peace, where connection to God and those we hold dear is so shaped by grace and mercy that we know and are known to a depth that would have frightened us when our hearts were smaller?

We need a garden in the midst of our busy, never-satisfied souls. We forge that place of rest when we embrace the message of the four gardens. The first garden comforts us: God's garden is a garden of richness. The second garden takes us to the place we are reluctant to enter, the place where we are called to die. The third garden opens the door to hope; God knows us by name and will make all things right. The fourth garden invites us to take up residence. We are called to live the life we have been given out of a garden heart where we are nourished, healed, and made fruitful as the life of Jesus flows through us.

As a young woman I was afraid of rest. I knew that in the silence, in the ceasing, in the letting go to which it called me, I could very well encounter fearful things inside my soul. I have indeed encountered those things. But in the process of embracing the first three garden places, I am being led to that garden in the midst of the city. The river that waters that garden is clear and deep; it both satisfies and makes me thirstier than I have ever been. The tree provides for my nourishment, enriching my heart and healing my broken places. In that city garden, I am learning the great gift of rest of heart.

Your story is different from mine, but your heart knows the same longings and fears. It knows the same seeming obstacles to rest. Soul turbulence visits you, and you face the temptation to believe that no rest can be yours until you've weathered the storm you find yourself in. Despite your longings for a full heart, a heart of peace, something is often wrong. People plague you. They demand so much, or you cannot forgive and forget their offenses. Perhaps life is gray and you find no joy in the present. Or your focus is stuck on what you don't have. You may be surrounded by your fears, or held captive to your sorrows. You may even feel that your soul will never escape the dark heaviness that has descended upon it.

Today may be your opportunity to choose to pursue rest in the midst of the battle you face. Can you take a break from all your trying; can you give thanks and celebrate the goodness of what is; can you allow the present to be imperfect? Will you let God—rather than fulfilling circumstances or a put-together heart—be the place you call home? If you do, the gate of rest will open to you.

Perhaps for you it's really not heart turbulence that keeps you from rest. Instead you have been mesmerized by our frenetic culture so that you are blindly following its directives toward more, more, more. Or maybe it's not the culture. It may be you. Rest is scary and you're not sure you really want it. Yet regardless of whether you point to our culture or to your own fears, the life you really long for will only flow from a full and spacious heart that has learned rest. The path to that sort of heart leads through four gardens: the garden where you admit how deep your longings are, the garden of dying, the garden where the risen Jesus meets you and calls you by name, and the garden nourished by the river of living water.

The voice of Jesus calls for you to begin that journey toward Him, toward rest. Listen as He turns toward you:

"Are you tired? Worn out? Burned out on religion? Come to me. Get away with me and you'll recover your life. I'll show you how to take a real rest. Walk with me and work with me—watch how I do it. Learn the unforced rhythms of grace. I won't lay anything heavy or ill-fitting on you. Keep company with me and you'll learn to live freely and lightly." (Matthew 11:28-30, MSG)

You'll recover your life. Walk with Him, right into your own heart. Watch Him turn all that troubles you into a gateway to rest. Walk with Him. Walk away from the press of the oughts and shoulds that crowd your heart and time. Walk with Him. Walk through the four gardens and find your way to that river. Walk with Him—you will find yourself and you will find His rest.

Taking Time

1. Walk through the four gardens.
   What have they taught you about rest?

   What fears do you have about any of these gardens?

   What does it mean for you to fully enter each one of these gardens?

2. In chapter 1 you finished the following statement. Now finish it once more: If my soul were truly at rest . . .

Jesus, I Am Resting, Resting

Jesus, I am resting, resting, in the joy of what Thou art;
I am finding out the greatness of Thy loving heart.
Thou hast bid me gaze upon Thee, and Thy beauty fills my soul,
For by Thy transforming power, Thou hast made me whole.

O how great Thy loving kindness, vaster, broader than the sea!
Oh how marvelous Thy goodness, lavished all on me!
Yes, I rest in Thee, Beloved, know what wealth of grace is Thine,
Know Thy certainty of promise, and have made it mine.

Simply trusting Thee, Lord Jesus, I behold Thee as Thou art,
And Thy love, so pure, so changeless, satisfies my heart;
Satisfies its deepest longings, meet, supplies, its every need,
Compasseth me round with blessings: Thine is love indeed!

Ever lift Thy face upon me as I work and wait for Thee;
Resting 'neath Thy smile Lord Jesus, earth's dark shadows flee.
Brightness of my Father's glory, sunshine of my Father's face,
Keep me ever trusting, resting; fill me with Thy grace.

JEAN S. PIGOT, 1876

Notes

CHAPTER 1: A GARDEN, A LONGING, A GATE
1. John K. Ryan, trans., *The Confessions of Saint Augustine* (Garden City, NY: Image Books, 1962), p. 43.
2. John of the Cross, *You Set My Spirit Free: Devotional Readings Arranged and Paraphrased by David Hazard* (Minneapolis, MN: Bethany, 1994), p. 109.

CHAPTER 3: THE LAND OF SHADOWS
1. Elizabeth Davis, *English Bread and Yeast Cookery* (Newton, MA: Biscuit Books, Inc., 1994), p. 92.

CHAPTER 4: THE GRUMBLE GRINDS ON
1. C. S. Lewis, *The Great Divorce* (San Francisco: HarperSanFrancisco, 2001), pp. 77-78.

CHAPTER 6: LISTENING TO MY TEARS
1. C. S. Lewis, *A Grief Observed* (New York: Bantam Books, 1976), p. 4.
2. Gerald Sittser, *A Grace Disguised* (Grand Rapids, MI: Zondervan, 1996), pp. 33-34.
3. Sittser, p. 154.
4. Sittser, pp. 179-180.

CHAPTER 7: LEFT IN THE DARKNESS
1. John of the Cross, *You Set My Spirit Free: Devotional Readings Arranged and Paraphrased by David Hazard* (Minneapolis, MN: Bethany, 1994), pp. 56-57.
2. C. S. Lewis, *The Horse and His Boy* (New York: Collier, 1970), pp. 158-159.
3. From *Why, O Lord?*, quoted in Reuben P. Job and Norman Shawchuck, *A Guide to Prayer for All God's People* (Nashville, TN: Upper Room Books, 1990), p. 295.

CHAPTER 8: FORGING A PLACE OF REST
1. Julian of Norwich, *I Promise You a Crown: Devotional Readings Arranged and Paraphrased by David Hazard* (Minneapolis, MN: Bethany, 1995), p. 82.

SALLY BREEDLOVE AND HER HUSBAND, STEVE, HAVE LIVED IN several cities in the United States and Canada during their thirty years in pastoral ministry and now make their home in Raleigh, North Carolina. Highly involved in writing curriculum, teaching women's Bible studies, and discipling women, she is also a speaker at large women's conferences and smaller leadership conferences both in North America and abroad. An active homemaker, hostess, and mother, Sally cultivates the life of her heart through a passion for reading, prayer, and contemplation, and through enjoying God as she hikes the Appalachian Mountains and listens to the waves on a sailboat in the Gulf of Mexico. She is the mother of five children, two of whom are married, and grandmother to one.

Sally Breedlove looks forward to speaking to other women at conferences and retreats. You may contact her at P.O. Box 52032, Raleigh, NC, 27612 or by e-mail at *sbreedlove@nc.rr.com*.